OF G-MEN
AND·EGGHEADS

published with aid of grant
Figure Foundation
reading the meaning of reader

OF G-MEN
AND EGGHEADS

THE FBI AND THE
NEW YORK
INTELLECTUALS

JOHN RODDEN

UNIVERSITY OF
ILLINOIS PRESS
Urbana, Chicago, and Springfield

CONTENTS

PREFACE

When I first broached the topic of this book to a friend years ago, a onetime *Partisan Review* editor who knew the subjects of this book personally, he registered surprise that the FBI had kept such distinguished critics under surveillance for quite some length of time. He had doubted the possibility, he said, for two reasons: first, because their influence was limited to a small circle of other intellectuals; second, and more important, because after their early, sometimes brief involvements with the Left, each figure spotlighted in my triptych—Lionel Trilling, Dwight Macdonald, and Irving Howe—became a fierce anti-Stalinist and anti-communist. (So too did Alfred Kazin, the fourth *Partisan Review* subject discussed in passing here.)

These circumstances turn the G-men's doggedly insistent if sporadic pursuit of this intellectual quartet into a bizarre, risible paradox and point to the twin themes of this book. First, the Bureau had a huge blind spot in dealing with the American Left and had trouble making even obvious distinctions. Second, FBI agents had an equally large mental block in dealing with that strange species, the intellectual.[1] Oddly, although agents occasionally conducted interviews, did physical surveillance, and clipped journalistic pieces about a suspect—sometimes assiduously combing press reports for tidbits about which political meetings he attended or which protest letters she signed—rarely did they do the obvious, which was to read what these writers actually wrote. That "oversight" accounts partly for a comic aspect to the pattern of amusing mix-ups and ludicrous misunderstandings that recur in the FBI files. More significantly, some real issues also emerge about domestic espionage during peacetime, especially concerning Americans whose main activity is the free expression of opinion rather than the seditious organization of revolution.

I have sought to take a balanced view of the surveillance issue, neither condemning it root and branch as invariably a violation of privacy and individual rights nor advocating wide latitude for internal spying on security grounds. I also do not mean to inflate the public significance of the intellectuals featured in this book or to exaggerate their individual or collective importance to the FBI. Each was under surveillance only intermittently, for relatively short periods of time, and the FBI eventually lost interest in all of them. For example, after years of reports leading to a dossier of some seven hundred pages, J. Edgar Hoover could not even remember who Macdonald was. Moreover, the periodic security checks of Howe and his family represented a dishonorable affront rather than a campaign of intimidation or persecution, as he would have acknowledged. And apart from his acquaintance with Whittaker Chambers, Trilling was less radical and of less concern to the FBI than either Macdonald or Howe, even though both Lionel and his wife, Diana, were briefly members of a communist front organization. Yet in the climate of fear and paranoia that gripped the Feds, especially throughout the Cold War era during the middle decades of the twentieth century, even Trilling accumulated a substantial file. Nonetheless, these case histories, particularly the Macdonald saga and its misadventures, prove absorbing as an exposé of FBI illusions, as a revealing spectacle of sophomoric blundering, or simply for the sheer incongruity of observing luftmenschen become the object of clumsy and misplaced official suspicion.

All this adds further interest to the book in three ways. First, the lives and works of these men are intrinsically engaging, even from this unlikely angle, since they were among the leading men of American letters of the mid-twentieth century. Second, these investigations were appallingly inept and misplaced, though they fell far short of evoking the atmosphere of a police state, as the men investigated well knew. Third, each case history highlights, perhaps surprisingly, a dramatic slice of history in which these men had cameo roles—the Hiss-Chambers trials (Trilling), the Smith Act and Red Scare (Howe), and the star-crossed White House Festival of the Arts (Macdonald). In this last case, a gala event held in June 1965 that witnessed a Vietnam-era gathering of cultural figures by the Johnson administration that was never tried again, I argue that this fiasco marks a Dreyfus-like watershed moment in American literary history, representing the definitive end of the tacit tradition of mutual cordiality between the art world and the state and heralding what has since indeed become a seemingly permanent alienation between liberal-Left intellectuals and power in America.

In short, *Of G-Men and Eggheads: The FBI and the New York Intellectuals* sheds light on Washington's official attitude toward American intellectuals and discloses above all the intelligence services' overwhelming ignorance of yet wariness toward leftist groups. The surveillance was modest compared to the vast amount of FBI spying during the 1950s and 1960s on New Left leaders, student activists, and major American authors such as Steinbeck and Hemingway. The Bureau's monitoring nevertheless possesses significance and value, not only because it is so unexpected but also because these figures were so firmly and outspokenly anti-communist. It shows us that the G-men could not distinguish radicals from Reds, ex-radicals from radicals, or intellectuals from activists.

Ironically, when it came to investigating intellectuals, the intelligence services proved utterly unintelligent. For all the interviews recorded, all the dossiers assembled, and all the miles and man-hours logged in pursuit of these particular intellectuals and others like them, the FBI failed to grasp countless elementary biographical and political facts that were readily and publicly available. If only an agent or two had sat still and done a bit of serious reading.

Yes, if only he had read some portion of their work.

OF G-MEN
AND EGGHEADS

PROLOGUE
THE TRADITION OF THE NEW

Why should we care about this history? Is it a mere curio for scholars and specialists? Or is it significant and pertinent in today's post-communist, digital, globalized age? Apart from the stories that the following chapters tell and the value of this history as a (however imperfect and impartial) record of what happened, one answer is that the past is *not* an entirely foreign country—and, in fact, is by no means even passed. For the new century in which we live was shaped by the Cold War era and can only be fully appreciated by understanding the developments of those decades. That history established the current conditions—not only political and social but also psychological—that govern the choices facing the United States and the rest of the world today.

Scholars have come to characterize the affinities between the Cold War and the War on Terror as the historical corridor "from 11/9 to 9/11."[1] That linkage reflects a perception that comparison of the epochs closing with the fall of the Berlin Wall on November 9, 1989, and opening with the collapse of New York City's Twin Towers on September 11, 2001, may help us better comprehend and meet our present-day challenges. The corridor metaphor alerts us to veiled interconnections between the two periods, impugning the trumpeted claim that 9/11 symbolized the dawning of an incommensurable brave new world of heightened uncertainty and insecurity.

That idea is headline-grabbing, but is it true? Did the attack at the World Trade Center really represent a rupture with the past, as the pundits and talking heads pronounced? Did it start an utterly different type of international conflict marked by a seismic shift from a clash of ideologies (capitalist versus communist) to a "clash of civilizations" (Western versus Islamic)?[2]

Every great "new" crisis is met initially with shock and angst that it is unheralded and unprecedented, that it has somehow mysteriously broken suddenly upon us. So it was with the Bolsheviks in the aftermath of World War I, with the fascists in the 1920s and 1930s, and with the guerrilla warfare of the Maoist-inspired North Vietnamese in the 1950s and 1960s.

We might call this geopolitical mirage the "tradition of the new." I say that because my research on the Cold War in preparation for this book convinces me that it is a myth that 9/11 changed the world. The notion that this "war" against terrorist organizations and rogue states is "new" lacks historical perspective. It is a truism no more valid than the celebrated declarations that "November 9" signified "The End of History"[3] and inaugurated a "New World Order"[4]—or, for that matter, that "1945" equaled "Year Zero,"[5] a reset of the historical clock, whereby tyrannical evil was slain by the forces of good and exclamations of "Nie wieder!" (Never again!) would forever replace the war cries.[6]

The "tradition of the new" is a venerable one.[7] And yet, beholden as it is to an ahistorical presentism, a tyranny of the immediate, it is also hazardous. We dare not toss the past "down the memory hole," as does Winston Smith in George Orwell's *Nineteen Eighty-Four*. For no war starts or ends in isolation. From World War I came the seeds of World War II. From World War II came the Cold War. Although influential neoconservative hawks in the George W. Bush administration declared "Islamofascism" a radically new, exceptional threat, leading the president to proclaim a fire-and-brimstone theology rather than craft a coherent strategy, even voices such as defense secretary Donald Rumsfeld believed that the so-called War on Terrorism would be waged "much like the Cold War." Indeed the Cold War is bound to have a profound impact on how America wages the War on Terror simply because the intelligence, bureaucratic, and military-industrial institutions that have shaped U.S. strategy since 9/11 took their present shape during the Cold War. Admittedly, dramatic differences between the circumstances of the Cold War era and the dangers confronting the twenty-first century prevail, among them the shifts from conventional to digital warfare and from ominous nation-states to "rogue" states and sects. But the respective challenges and constraints shared by the two periods also possess notable similarities.

Both the obvious discontinuities and the more subtle continuities with the recent past require judicious assessment from us today. For example, just as American leaders before World War II needed to "unlearn" the lessons of isolationism in the 1930s to fight World War II, American policymakers today need to unlearn the lessons of conventional warfare—including "intelligence" warfare—to combat rogue states and terrorist cells in the twenty-first century.

This brief study of U.S. Cold War intelligence possesses implications for these large issues, especially the ever-vexing dilemma of the responsible balance between protecting civil liberties and defending national security. Engaging them from the vantage point of how the Federal Bureau of Investigation (FBI) conducted surveillance on a trio of leftist literary intellectuals,[8] the study opens with an introductory chapter that raises the broad questions and indicates how the succeeding case histories address them. Drawing heavily on declassified FBI dossiers of the principals, each of the next three chapters narrates in sharp detail a slice of Cold War intellectual history, concluding with some reflections on each case's wider contemporary significance.

I do not claim that this (or any other) work of history yields direct historical "analogies" and/or possesses explicit historical "lessons." As I argue in the Epilogue, I do indeed believe, however, that careful dialogue with the "past not yet passed" can assist us as we contemplate the extant and emergent conflicts on the world stage in our own time.[9] For the Cold War generation confronted the same basic conflict between freedom and security that continues to perplex us. Many of the Orwellian terrors currently associated with lawless violence by states and sects and by cyberwarfare through megaviruses and digital worms had their respective geopolitical and technological origins during the "crucial decade" following World War II.[10]

All espionage activities represent a flawed answer to the freedom-versus-liberty dilemma. Still, FBI director J. Edgar Hoover regarded radicals such as those featured in these pages as a political plague, a contagion rapidly spreading in the early Cold War era and threatening to infect the lifeblood of the American body politic. It was a secondary matter to him that these men were American citizens, with constitutional rights that their government should have felt obliged to safeguard. That Hoover's anti-communist obsession and McCarthyist incursions on civil rights never remotely approached the Orwellian horrors of Stalin's NKVD (secret police) and gulag owes in large part to the fact that Cold War America, its substantial failings notwithstanding, struck a more or less fair balance between the Scylla and Charybdis of liberty and security. Unlike the deep freeze that prevailed from the 1930s through the mid-1950s in the USSR, the American political climate was chilly, which resulted in serious and deplorable infringements on civil liberties yet did not remotely approach a Big Brother police state.

Nonetheless, Hoover's agents were often insufficiently scrupulous in their respect for the civil liberties of all American citizens, including "egghead" leftist intellectuals. The Bureau's less-than-strenuous exertions to defend the basic rights of politically engaged Americans have had far-reaching impact. Some of the most recent outcomes can be witnessed in the wake of Edward

Snowden's disclosures in May 2013 of government intelligence programs that collect millions of telephone records and track Internet activity.[11] Whistle-blowers such as Snowden have done what the intellectuals in this study were not in a position to do: expose the details of the government's "almost Orwellian" practice of "un-American" mass surveillance of American citizens.[12]

In an uncertain world featuring ever-present nuclear, digital, and terrorist threats to global and natural security—as well as unpredictably shifting great power rivalries (à la George Orwell's geopolitical scenario in *Nineteen Eighty-Four*!)—competent, high-performing intelligence agencies are a (reluctant) state necessity. That is especially true for a superpower such as America. But intelligence operations must abide by the U.S. Constitution and Bill of Rights, not by the preferences of intelligence agency heads, let alone secret courts and faceless bureaucrats in some obscure netherworld or dim shadowland beyond public inspection.

All this is even more imperative in a century during which advances in surveillance technologies render certain aspects of old-fashioned snooping by J. Edgar Hoover's G-men almost quaint by comparison. Still, if some technical issues have changed, what has not—and must not be—changed is our commitment to fulfilling our national security objectives while preserving our civic liberties. Although the balance will always be imperfect, freedom and security *are* reconcilable—a both/and, not a versus or an either/or. A democratic government *can* safeguard the nation without resorting to the methods of the dictators and terrorists we battle.

The Epilogue ends and elaborates on that note. We need not scotch National Security Agency data-dragnet programs designed to expose terrorist networks or scuttle FBI initiatives to uncover possible plans of domestic terrorism. Rather, we must *watch* our intelligence services "intelligently"— that is, through "watchdog" policies with sharp teeth that mandate rigorous congressional monitoring, periodic judicial review, independent outside examination and reporting, and regular legislative evaluation.

As we aspire to balance and harmonize the security screams with the freedom chants, good statesmanship and citizenship demand a measured response whereby we blend the innovative with the orthodox. If we are to address change responsibly, we must ponder the pertinence of tradition as we engage the permutations of the new.

CHAPTER ONE

INTELLECTUALS AND INTELLIGENCE SERVICES

THE *PARTISAN REVIEW* WRITERS UNDER THE WATCHFUL EYE OF THE FBI

> Eggheads of the world unite—you have
> nothing to lose but your yolks.
> —Adlai Stevenson, 1958

> You can't make an omelet without
> breaking eggheads.
> —Adlai Stevenson, 1961 (attributed)

THE BANALITY OF INTELLIGENCE?

This book might easily have been titled *The Banality of "Intelligence."*[1] Unlike many previous studies of the relationship between U.S. security agencies and American writers and intellectuals, these pages contain neither shocking revelations of privacy invasion nor disgusted expressions of antinomian outrage, voiced either by the author or by the principals themselves. Instead, this compact study represents a story about the conduct of official American security activities in terms of what, following Thomas Kuhn, I call "normal Intelligence." By that phrase I mean that the book reflects the utterly ordinary, repetitive, even grindingly tedious snooping so frequently and so stupidly involved in purported "intelligence gathering" conducted upon Americans suspected of posing "national security risks." The primary conclusion of the book is that the routine collection of such data ("normal Intelligence") by the Federal Bureau of Investigation (FBI), particularly during the Cold War decades, was all too often unwarranted, pointless, wasteful, and needless.[2]

In a word: banal. Utterly banal.

Such practices by the FBI and other intelligence services have given rise to the caricatures and jokes captured by the book's main title and epigraphs. The files discussed in this study, along with almost every other government dossier that I have seen, support that conclusion, for the Americans profiled in these chapters never figured as national security risks. And that is just the point. This study's ultimate lesson constitutes a very simple, cautionary admonition: let us exercise restraint when it comes to expending valuable resources on government spying, especially on American citizens, under the pretense of safeguarding "internal security." American security officials need to practice greater care, for even if no obvious harm is done to a subject's career or personal or professional relationships, the sheer effrontery of invading citizens' privacy (and usually that of their families and friends) is sufficient reason to insist on strict limits and public vigilance.

This book focuses on the leading members of the elder generation of radicals known as the New York Intellectuals: Lionel Trilling, Dwight Macdonald, and Irving Howe.[3] All of them wrote for *Partisan Review* (*PR*), the premier literary-political quarterly in the United States from the mid-1930s through the mid-1960s. This little magazine formed the publishing hub for this circle of chiefly Jewish, nonacademic, freelance New York writers. In *Lionel Trilling and the Critics* (1999), *The Worlds of Irving Howe* (2005), *Irving Howe and the Critics* (2005), and *Politics and the Intellectual: Conversations with Irving Howe* (2010), I have devoted extensive and detailed attention to this important group of intellectuals, which also included such prominent cultural voices as Sidney Hook, Diana Trilling, Philip Rahv, Mary McCarthy, Hannah Arendt, Alfred Kazin, Irving Kristol, and Norman Podhoretz, all of whom also appear in the pages of this book.[4]

The following chapters are based on original, unpublished research materials, primarily FBI reports and memoranda obtained through the Freedom of Information Act. In addition, I have expanded the book's scope by making selective use of archival holdings at the Harry Ransom Center at the University of Texas at Austin—particularly the collections of Nicolas Nabokov and Michael Josselson, both of whom were administrators of the Congress for Cultural Freedom, an organization founded in 1950 under the auspices of the State Department to fight Stalinism on the cultural front.[5] I have focused on how FBI surveillance of the first generation of New York Intellectuals—in particular Trilling, Macdonald, and Howe—subjected them to close government attention between the 1930s and 1970s.[6] These three men arguably were the most central and influential members of the senior generation of *PR* writers,[7] and the often inept and ignorant treatment they experienced at the hands of the Feds accounts for my tongue-in-cheek epigraphs, which thematize the study's title, *Of G-Men and Eggheads: The FBI and the New York Intellectuals*.

VESTED INTERESTS AND GEOPOLITICAL POKER

What is spying? And what is gained by those government activities shrouded in secrecy that we term "intelligence gathering"? On the evidence in the following pages, a good deal of government surveillance proves costly and wasteful, represents a morally corrupt business of minimal practical value, and indeed often amounts to a comedy of errors.

I do not mean to indulge in the old joke, "Government intelligence is a contradiction in terms." Serious, respectable students of diplomacy and geopolitics have frequently argued that in the world of realpolitik, policymaking decisions in international relations and domestic security are necessarily often guided (or driven) by veiled, capricious motives or forces, many of which are not (and even perhaps should not) be fully available to the view of outsiders.[8]

So although my own view tends toward the skeptical and vigilant side of the matter, I do not want to exclude or ridicule the opposing position or imply that secret intelligence gathering is always wasteful and worthless. But I do believe that *foreign* intelligence gathering (i.e., pertaining to foreign citizens abroad), especially in wartime, is most defensible. *Domestic* surveillance of American citizens is a much more questionable activity, especially in peacetime. The material in this book deals chiefly with domestic intelligence gathering regarding American intellectuals, most of it collected during the Cold War decade spanning the mid-1940s to the mid-1950s—that is, from the immediate post–World War II era to the so-called Red Scare of the McCarthy years.[9] In my view, such domestic intelligence activity is far more dubious than spying practices by the Central Intelligence Agency (CIA) and other agencies abroad, especially during World War II or the conflicts in Korea and Vietnam.

Some of the activities of the Office of Strategic Service (OSS) during World War II certainly contributed to the safety of Allied soldiers and, to some extent, even if the consequences were not decisive, to the Allies' ultimate victory in the war. And most other international powers besides the United States also have engaged in espionage in the belief that nations both require information about other governments to conduct their affairs and are obliged, in a world of conflict and strife, to hide some of their policymaking rationales from military and economic adversaries. International politics is a matter of "game theory," even high-stakes poker, whereby rival government "players" seek to know what military-economic cards their opponents hold while striving to keep their own hands away from opponents' eyes. Such geopolitical realities as existed during the Cold War decades support the realpolitik attitudes of diplomatic thinkers ranging from Metternich and Bismarck to Hans Morgenthau and Henry Kissinger—that is, a neo-Machiavellian stance that could be rubricated by that famous, cynical pronouncement in *The Prince*: "Princes" (or "princ-ipalities"—i.e., kingdoms and nations) must have no friends, "only vested interests."[10] Yet here again we are talking about *foreign* policy and rival *nations*, not domestic matters and internal security policy.

Most national security policymakers believe that advantages accrue precisely whenever they know the "hand" dealt to their opponents and can keep their own cards close to their vest. To know what resources their adversaries command, how they might deploy those resources, and what determines their motives and purposes—these are the principal aims behind spying. As H. S. Ferns, a prominent British scholar and former security analyst for Whitehall, explained the government's position in a widely cited and still-pertinent statement,

> It follows from all this that there is a pressing need for informed debate on all these complex and difficult issues; but it is a debate that requires to be conducted in good faith by those who wish to reach sensible conclusions. Those who merely want to drive discussion into a series of blind alleys should, if possible, be ignored if not excluded. Just as there are those who so mistrust nuclear weapons that they pretend these can be disinvented, so there are some so hostile to secrecy and to Secret Services that they would like to abolish both. In a perfect world, freedom of information would have no bounds; in the world that we inhabit it is a question of striking the right balance. . . .
>
> The cooperation of all sensible men is needed if [critics' claims] of excessive secrecy and excessive speculation [are] to be dispelled in a constructive manner. Ignorance has always been the ally of rumour and prejudice. We have had quite enough of both.[11]

These conservative views run counter to my own.[12] Yet they deserve a hearing and should be heeded by government critics as well as official policymakers.

THE UNGENTLEMANLY "SPY BUSINESS"

Baldly asserted without qualification, then, the "banality of 'Intelligence'" is a misconceived and rash overgeneralization that we should avoid. My own position is that intelligence work possesses primary value when it is conducted against foreign governments or on foreign nationals and, indeed, when other channels of information are insufficiently reliable or somehow compromised. Espionage is most justifiable when other, public sources of information (including above all the mass media) cannot inform policymakers adequately to make reliable decisions. One of the major difficulties with all intelligence data, as I discovered again and again during my research in the secret police archives of the former East Germany (the so-called Stasi files kept on both dissidents and ordinary citizens), is an overwhelming superabundance of information. East German policymakers and Stasi administrators ultimately were paralyzed, drowning in an ocean of random bits of data obtained from informants, wiretaps, electronic bugging, and so on. They could not distinguish the significant from the trivial in a multitude of cases.[13] This problem is well known both to the intelligence agencies and the policymaking officials who seek to use the data.

Why, then, do governments insist on supporting the activities of the security agencies? The reason is not so much because the information is likely to be objectively accurate or reliable, but rather—if not trustworthy in its accuracy—it is at minimum trustworthy in its source. (This assumes, of course, that the source is not a double agent.) Since advanced technology cannot obtain some kinds of information (and in any case needs to be interpreted by trustworthy experts), the old-fashioned spy still has a role to play from the standpoint of government decision-making.[14] He is "our man in Havana," to cite the brilliant novel by Graham Greene.[15] We would not expect the U.S. government to rely on Russian or Chinese intelligence agents any more than we would rely on their mass media or other official sources of information. Governments want information that they can trust, at least insofar as personal relationships may heighten the likelihood that this information is reliable. As Ferns wrote during the mid-1980s, at the dawn of the Gorbachev era and just a few years before the fall of the Berlin Wall, "The important point is that the Soviet authorities wanted information they could trust, and they wanted 'their boy' to acquire it. They could trust it, not because it was necessarily better information than they could gain out of standard books and reports, but because they had the loyalty of, and control over, the one providing it. This was the political ingredient which made the information operational for them."[16]

Why has the United States always had a more open stance toward intelligence gathering—a form of so-called American exceptionalism? Aside from our fortunate constitutional and legislative history, along with a tradition of and public support for an "open society," the main reason is that Washington is a comparative "latecomer to the spy business" and its "ungentlemanly" ways:

Until World War II [American policymakers] disdained the methods of the decadent old states of Europe who ran makeshift clandestine operations in foreign communities and in their own colonies. ("Gentlemen," said Henry L. Stimson, "don't read other gentlemen's mail. . . .") The FBI ran an intelligence operation directed against "criminals and subversives" in the United States in the 1930s, and the U.S. Army and Navy developed intelligence work for military purposes; but it was World War II and its aftermath which prompted them to establish clandestine political work. True to their national aptitudes, the Americans jumped into the business with enthusiasm and great faith in their technological capacities. They learned from the British, and they imitated the Soviets; they also spent a heap of money on personnel and gadgetry—with what success it is hard to judge.[17]

Relatively speaking, the United States has represented a notable exception to the prevailing habit among international powers to keep all knowledge about intelligence-gathering activities concealed from their own citizens and media. The U.S. Constitution, along with other American legislation, guarantees that U.S. government intelligence activity will be revealed in detail in the course of time. It is not readily admitted by critics of the U.S. government (e.g., Noam Chomsky) that our intelligence activities are far less secretive and far more open than those of the Russians (even today, let alone during the Soviet era). In fact, U.S. intelligence activities are considerably more open than those of even our allies, whether in London or Paris or Berlin or Tel Aviv.

In fact, this volume—like most books that have discussed the activities of U.S. security agencies—could not have been written without "open government" legislation, such as the Freedom of Information Act (FOIA). Most of the dossiers quoted in this book were obtained through the FOIA, even if many of the files that I received contained numerous pages that have been heavily redacted (or "blacked out") allegedly because they allude to persons still living or to national security matters still considered sensitive. (In some instances, I was allowed on appeal to see parts of these files with fewer pages blacked out after a special review process permitted by the FOIA departments of all agencies.)

Indeed the FOIA makes it possible to write books such as this one, which is a far more difficult undertaking in other nations. Thanks to the FOIA, Americans can learn a great deal about U.S. government intelligence work. Moreover, we can debate, for example, whether policies such as waterboarding alleged terrorists in Afghanistan or Iraq is defensible in light of criteria from CIA handbooks or State Department policymaking documents.[18] Our traditions of civic participation and public dissent, characterized by a broad, popular consensus that political decisions necessarily include ethical considerations, account for these "sunshine laws" as well as for our distinctiveness among major powers in our legislative restrictions on espionage, both today and during the Cold War. As Ferns has written,

> American discussion of their intelligence work (and of clandestine political activities directed at foreign states) tends to concentrate on the morality of the business, not on whether it is successful or otherwise. Whether bad intelligence work and inept clandestine politics can account for the American disasters in Cuba, Viet Nam, the Middle East, and the present difficulties in Central America, are questions not easy to answer, and perhaps impossible. Obviously American misjudgment in these areas has been massive and disastrous, but it is not necessary to accept the Soviet/Marxist arguments that events in Cuba, etc., are a manifestation of the inevitability of history *à la* Marx. Rather than accept that history is not on our side, we need to ask ourselves: what are we doing wrong?[19]

NATIONAL SECURITY VERSUS CIVIL LIBERTIES

Even more insistently, we need to ask ourselves another, rather different question. Why did Cold War–era intellectuals—a tiny grouplet of American citizenry without much political power but with some cultural visibility—invite such close attention from the FBI and other security agencies? Once again, historical timing largely determines the answer. The middle decades of the twentieth century were a period of ideological ferment. Complex and shifting political relationships were the order of the day, especially among Left intellectuals. As Ferns notes,

> The "United Front" tactics of the 1930s involved clandestine domination of the Left everywhere by Communist Parties loyal to Stalinism. Nowadays the slogan "No enemies on the Left" means an acceptance of, and collaboration with, Trotskyists, democratic socialists, revolutionary nationalists, hippy bombsters and even romantic anarchists. "Broad Left" alliances, Militant Tendencies, Euro-Communism, etc., are all acceptable vehicles on the road to destabilisation of the bourgeois-capitalist enemies. The Soviet politicians are able to adopt this "liberal" line because the Soviet state is now firmly established, its police methods are comprehensive, and its armed forces are large and technically well-equipped. They take the long view—confident that when circumstances are right they can do away with their allies as Lenin did with his in 1918–23. Keeping the pot of revolution boiling is more important than doctrinal orthodoxy.[20]

Of course, the "long view" was summarily axed two decades ago by the harsh tribunal of history—and the USSR, like East Germany, no longer even exists. Yet the West remains. And regardless of the antagonists we face, whether the Cold War Russians or the "rogue state" terrorists, our ultimate preoccupations should not alter. Our interest should focus on how to balance and reconcile the security of the state and the rights of the individual. Both priorities are vital to political and social democracy.[21]

So how can they be balanced and reconciled? International tensions (especially in Afghanistan and Iraq), recurrent security scandals, and the astounding progress in surveillance technology (e.g., American drone aircraft) keep controversies and disputes about all types of spying in the headlines. These dilemmas of balance should be part of public discussion and debate. To some extent, the United States remains far ahead of other major powers in this respect. American legislators, and to a lesser extent the American media, have discussed such matters since the CIA was founded in 1947. Various congressional committees, especially since the mid-1970s (e.g., the Church Committee, chaired by Senator Frank Church), forthrightly debated the relevant issues. A permanent Select Committee on Intelligence has subsequently been established. Accompanying legislation from that period, including the FOIA and the Foreign Intelligence Surveillance Act (FISA), have benefited research scholars like myself immensely.

Not until the 1990s did Great Britain and most other European countries have any formal legislation governing aspects of domestic surveillance such as wiretapping and electronic bugging. The British Parliament has never exercised close supervision over its secret services. The U.K. Security Commission possesses the power to do so, but it is an executive agency that generally limits its activities to inquiries into errors or human rights abuses. By and large, the British practice has been to leave all policymaking to the Home Office, an executive agency comparable in its jurisdiction to a combination of the Departments of Homeland Security and Justice.[22]

American citizens should be especially wary about allowing domestic surveillance of suspected "subversives." Our concern should not only involve the danger of security agencies exceeding their powers illegally. Elastic, often expansive guidelines (such as the Patriot Act under the Bush administration) are easily abused. Lawmakers should exert extreme care when crafting espionage legislation and practicing administration oversight. They should especially scrutinize the fine and often blurred line between breaking laws and keeping a watchful eye on potential troublemakers. If surveillance is conducted under lawful authority and with proper safeguards, I regard it as legitimate to investigate American citizens whose activities lead to reasonable suspicion that they are endangering our national security.

As we shall see, the three key members of the senior generation of New York Intellectuals who are profiled in this book never posed any such threat.

That fact might seem at first glance to represent a disabling disadvantage for this study, as if implying, "So what is the point? Is this just a 'nonstudy,' a study in negation?" Not at all. The cases of these three intellectuals raise numerous relevant political and historical issues and exemplify the daily round of "normal Intelligence," thereby illustrating the general rule rather than the infrequent exception. If their dossiers are less action-packed or juicy than those of some acknowledged victims (e.g., Ernest Hemingway, whom Trilling admired and envied for daring to become a "writer," not a mere "critic"), the distinct advantage is that the files of these *PR* writers accurately reflect routine FBI practices and their outcomes. An additional advantage is that each of the three dossiers features one key episode that forms its centerpiece and independently raises significant political questions—for example, Trilling's novel *The Middle of the Journey* for its personal and literary connections to Whittaker Chambers, Macdonald's attendance at the 1965 White House Festival of the Arts, and Howe's interview by FBI agents shortly after he founded *Dissent* in 1954.

Moreover, quite apart from these considerations, to scrutinize the dossiers of the senior generation of *PR* writers offers distinct advantages that derive from the historical fact that this was the only prominent post–World War II group of intellectuals to emerge in America. Thus the book possesses not only a group-centered coherence but also—given the differences among Trilling, Macdonald, and Howe—a diversity and depth that such a tightly focused study would otherwise lack.

This diversity includes the interesting fact that the files directly mirror the personalities of these three men. The Trilling chapter is unsensational, as if deliberately circumspect and self-controlled, a Bureau tableau of a figure who sometimes strikes me as *Partisan Review*'s "Man without Qualities."[23] By contrast, the Macdonald chapter is virtually the polar opposite of its predecessor. If the monochromatic Trilling file is a paleface portrait in sepia, Macdonald's dossier represents its motley, brightly colored, even iridescent counterpart. Befitting the man himself, Macdonald's file is full of comedy and slapstick, reflecting his own love of high jinks, showmanship, and storytelling.

Quite different from both the Trilling and Macdonald dossiers are Howe's FBI records. Echoing Howe's earnest, righteous (sometimes self-righteous) temperament, his dossier reads as a straightforward public document: Howe the socialist tribune and dissenting intellectual, under FBI scrutiny as a potentially dangerous ideologue and revolutionary. Civic issues of reason and principle, fairness and justice, moral and legal authority, and rights and responsibilities echo throughout Howe's dossier. Unlike the Macdonald file, it is bereft of quirky, personal detail. Still, it is absorbingly readable in its own way.

As one who has studied the lives and written extensively about the work of this trio of New York Intellectuals, I am amused and fascinated by the (uncanny) parallels between their dossiers and their public images and personal temperaments: the Bufile as profile. (The term *Bufile* was shorthand for "Bureau file" in FBI jargon.)

Or as Macdonald, an irrepressible punster and a devotee of repartee, might have riffed on his loudly proclaimed conviction that prose style mirrored lifestyle (*Le style c'est l'homme*), "The File is the man." (Or at his most Dwighteously indignant, "The Boo-file is the G-man.")

SHADOWING LIONEL TRILLING

If you dabbled in left-wing politics at virtually any time during the two decades before and after World War II, you could be certain of one thing—J. Edgar Hoover's FBI was maintaining a dossier on you. This does not imply that the Bureau's snooping was justified. It merely means that it was inevitable.

Lionel Trilling (1905–75) has often been regarded as the leader and most influential member of the New York Intellectuals and in fact has been paired with Edmund Wilson as the foremost American cultural critic of the twentieth century. Much has been written about Trilling—including a half dozen substantial critical studies and scores of scholarly articles—but no attention has yet been devoted to how he was viewed in official government circles and by their clandestine intelligence services. The FBI dossier on Trilling provides an opportunity to see how he was regarded behind the scenes.

Although Trilling was never aggressively pursued by the Bureau, his dossier contains valuable and revealing historical material. Among other things, his file discloses how out of touch FBI intelligence was about which American intellectuals posed security threats—and how misplaced was Trilling's increasing satisfaction with post-war American life.

As in the case of FBI surveillance of Howe, the Jewish context of the Trilling investigation is an open question that is difficult to answer. The FBI clearly was especially interested in Jewish intellectuals, including many of the older *PR* writers, because of their communist (specifically Trotskyist) backgrounds or convictions. Trilling's parents were from Białystok in Poland, which until the Polish-Soviet War of 1919–20 (and again after 1939) lay in Russia. The immigration of such Russian Jews into the United States often raised eyebrows, particularly among those FBI agents who were not informed about the various social factors that led to the influx of Russian-speaking Jews into the country. My research into the FBI investigations of Trilling and Howe convinces me that the Jewish dimension was a factor in the FBI's interest, though probably not a decisive one.

The existence of an FBI dossier on Trilling stems chiefly from his short-lived 1930s political activity, which ceased by the beginning of World War II, though he maintained friendly or collegial relations with numerous subjects of FBI searches. Trilling himself was seldom the focus of an FBI probe; rather, his name emerged in connection with major figures under FBI investigation. The file discloses how even a relatively unpolitical man such as Trilling, as a prominent intellectual associated with numerous radical writers and thinkers and also on the fringes of subversive political organizations during his youth, comes to be connected to some of the great political issues of his time and inevitably attracts the attention of the Bureau. The FBI dossier thus traces the shadow life, as it were, of Trilling's fading connections with communism beyond his formal association with communists and their activities in the early 1930s.

DWIGHT MACDONALD, ALWAYS ADAMANTLY "AGAINST THE (UN-)AMERICAN GRAIN"

Dwight Macdonald (1906–82)—rather like George Orwell, with whom he corresponded extensively—was a political radical yet a cultural conservative. He would have agreed with Orwell that "the slovenliness of our language makes it easier for us to have foolish thoughts."[24] Macdonald's essays bemoaning the faddish modernized revisions of the King James Bible, the turgid prose of Mortimer Adler's A Syntopicon (1952), and the jargon-laden rhetoric of Vice President Henry Wallace all reflected his well-justified contempt for lax and slipshod prose. He was a cultural conservative in literary matters insofar as he fought to preserve the canons of English usage and the traditions and norms of literary excellence. In these respects, Macdonald serves as a model and mentor for independent-minded intellectuals today. Yet his ideological follies—which point to the yawning gap between him and Orwell in terms of political acumen and intellectual legacy—are impossible to overlook.

Macdonald's proud inconsistencies and instinctive antinomianism flummoxed FBI agents. Yet these paradoxes (or outright contradictions) kept the Feds, dogged if confused, on his case. For example, Macdonald's celebration of the counterculture of the 1960s extended even to enthusiasm for the Yippies and for the student demonstrators who occupied professors' offices and closed down colleges. Such positions both baffled the FBI and illustrate how Macdonald's inveterate iconoclasm undermined the very traditions and norms of excellence that he otherwise championed.

It is unsurprising that the FBI, whose agents were seldom versed in the details of internecine warfare within the sectarian Left—let alone in the nuances of left-wing intellectual debates—did not comprehend such a nonpareil individualist as Macdonald. Yes, he had been an enthusiast for Trotsky and briefly a member of the Socialist Workers Party, a Trotskyist sect, during the mid-1930s. Yet he was no "un-American"—not before, during, or after the McCarthy years of the early 1950s. FBI agents failed to appreciate how he was indeed a "Critical American," if not a "Good American" (in his phrases).[25] They failed to appreciate how his stance "against the American grain" (in his 1962 essay collection of that title) steadfastly maintained critical support for the United States.[26] They failed to appreciate the value of his libertarian vision, especially his trenchant critiques in *Partisan Review* and *politics* of both liberalism and totalitarianism.

Macdonald is best described as a "Critical American" who was, above all, "against the *un*-American grain." All this notwithstanding, if he had ever had the opportunity to inspect his substantial FBI dossier, this seasoned veteran of internecine Left sectarian warfare would have proudly brandished his files of yesteryear as a badge of honor.

IRVING HOWE, LIFELONG *DISSENTER*

The FBI dossier on Irving Howe (1920–93) proves that the concerns that he voiced in *Dissent* about the sorry state of American civic life during the 1950s and early 1960s were well founded.[27] His wife was subjected to investigation during her years as a teacher at Miss Fine's Day School in Princeton, New Jersey. His lectures and seminars were attended by FBI agents or informants, his mail was checked repeatedly, and his personal information (physical characteristics, children, residence, phone numbers, car model) was monitored.[28] The FBI justified these intrusions into Howe's personal life on the basis of his longtime membership in a Trotskyist sect, the Shachtmanites (headed by Max Shachtman), in which Howe became active at the age of eighteen (after entering the Young People's Socialist League at thirteen) in the late 1930s and from which he formally withdrew in 1952.

Why did such youthful Trotskyist activities prompt the Feds to investigate Howe? FBI paranoia and ignorance played a large role. It was as if the G-men believed that the tiny worlds of Trotskyist parties really did pose some enormous threat to American security and the national welfare. At times the FBI's ignorance was sovereign, extending so far as to imagine that various Trotskyist sects—whose membership totals often barely reached three figures nationally—formed a crucial part of a Soviet beachhead inside American borders. This idea represents an incredible, glaring absurdity in light of the fact that Stalin hated and vilified Trotsky so much that his GPU (secret police) agents hounded him all the way to Mexico and then murdered him. Did an FBI agent ever really listen for just a few minutes to the harangues at a typical Trotskyist meeting of the 1940s? One wonders. Any agent who did so would have acquired irrefutable testimony that the most dyed-in-the-wool, one-note, anti-Soviet (and, of course, anti-Stalinist) dogmatists had found a home together. It was a home perfectly suited to luftmensch dialecticians and doctrinal purists—that is, to unworldly Marxist intellectuals.

Yet evidence of such testimony never surfaces in any of these three men's files or in other similar dossiers that I have examined, such as Alfred Kazin's. Instead the prosaic, plodding FBI agents at such meetings scented global danger, beholden to the delusion that a few dozen leaderless Trotskyist utopians constituted a "revolutionary vanguard" poised to overthrow the U.S. government. Or as if FBI agents really believed Adlai Stevenson's bon mot: "Eggheads of the world unite—you have nothing to lose but your yolks." Indeed it was as if the Bureau's irrational anxiety fed on another Stevenson witticism, "You can't make an omelet without breaking eggheads."[29]

Nonetheless, despite the FBI's extensive and intrusive surveillance of his private life, Howe never engaged in so-called McCarthy-baiting—that is, he did not equate domestic infringements on American's civil liberties during McCarthyism with the Soviet gulag. In *A Margin of Hope*, Howe grants that the McCarthy era was no "reign of terror." "In a reign of terror," he writes, "people turn silent, fear a knock on the door at 4 in the morning, flee in all directions; but they do not, because they cannot, talk endlessly in public about the outrage of terror." Referring to the radical-liberal journal of opinion that he founded in the mid-1950s and edited until his death forty years later, he adds, "When we printed violent denunciations of McCarthy in *Dissent* during these years, nothing happened to us. . . . [W]e had no sense we were taking any great risks in attacking McCarthy."[30]

Howe's treatment by the Bureau may not be a case study in political repression, but Americans of the twenty-first century should remain vigilant about political stupidities like this one. The FBI's pursuit of Howe was intolerable and unnecessary; it demonstrated a skewed understanding of the balance among national security, social order, and personal liberty. Such "routine" snooping—the practice of gratuitous, irrelevant, invasive surveillance—is what anyone concerned about Americans' civil liberties and the right to "dissent" must vigorously protest—not just yesterday but also today.

Lionel Trilling in the 1960s in his office in Philosophy Hall at Columbia University, where he taught for more than thirty years.

Courtesy: University Archives, Columbia University, in the City of New York

CHAPTER TWO

AN UNLIKELY SUSPECT

LIONEL TRILLING, STALINIST FELLOW TRAVELER?

THE SPY WHO NEVER WAS

The Federal Bureau of Investigation (FBI) never conducted a formal investigation of Lionel Trilling.[1] But the FBI dossier on Trilling discloses that the Bureau followed his activities intermittently for almost three decades, periodically searching his records, interviewing him to uncover information about his acquaintances, and investigating him as a possible security risk long after he had resigned from the National Committee for the Defense of Political Prisoners (NCDPP), a Communist Party (CP) affiliate organization consisting largely of writers and intellectuals.[2] The FBI files comprise sixty pages exclusively about him and include more than two hundred pages involving other investigations in which his name arose, prompting agents to monitor him.[3] The dossier runs from 1937 to 1965 and covers reports from regional FBI offices in New York City, Boston, Detroit, and Baltimore, though numerous pages are blacked out or redacted; most concern the Alger Hiss–Whittaker Chambers case.

Most of these reports address Trilling's peripheral connection to ongoing FBI probes and to its scrutiny of communist figures and issues, ranging from Leon Trotsky and his connections to sectarian American Trotskyist groups in the 1930s to the Soviet Union's anti-Semitism and the U.S. embargo against Castro's Cuba in the 1950s and 1960s. Much of the file addresses Trilling's novel, *The Middle of the Journey* (1947), because one of its protagonists, ex-CP member Gifford Maxim, was closely based on Whittaker Chambers, whom Trilling knew personally from their student days together at Columbia in the

Diana Trilling in her fifties.
Courtesy: University Archives,
Columbia University

early 1920s.[4] The file lays bare the inadequate modus operandi of certain FBI practices, exposing the bulky and ill-fitting nature of off-the-rack uniform routines in the standard data collection methods of secret intelligence agencies—especially when it comes to that top-heavy, asymmetrical creature, the intellectual. Defying basic common sense, no agent ever seems to have read any of Trilling's work to ascertain his political positions, except for what one agent refers to as the Bureau's "review" of Trilling's novel to determine whether it contained any useful information on Chambers's communist past. The agent determined that it did not. Chambers had tried to recruit both Trilling and his wife, Diana, for Soviet espionage. In her 1993 memoir, *The Beginning of the Journey: The Marriage of Diana and Lionel Trilling*, she candidly reports that she was proud to be asked, and although she refused, she felt sufficiently beholden to Chambers and the revolutionary cause that she never phoned the FBI.[5]

The Bureau never seriously harassed Lionel Trilling. Nonetheless, his dossier constitutes important historical material. Among other things, as I mentioned in the Introduction, his file makes clear that the FBI's intermittent attention to him was not only misplaced but also represented a poor use of government resources.

What role, if any, did Trilling's Jewishness play in arousing the FBI's interest in him? It is hard to say. Numerous other intellectuals coming of age in the 1930s and 1940s possessed similar immigrant backgrounds, including several other members of the *Partisan Review* group of Jewish intellectuals in New York City. FBI investigations of other Jewish intellectuals in New York make it likely that his Jewishness played some role, especially given that Trilling had served as assistant editor of *Menorah Journal* in the 1920s and 1930s. The FBI probably compiled a dossier on Trilling because he briefly joined a Communist front organization during the mid-1930s and was an acquaintance during his college years at Columbia of fellow classmate Whittaker Chambers.

A FELLOW TRAVELER'S JOURNEY ABANDONED

An active file was maintained on Trilling from the late 1930s to the mid-1960s. The file was updated when his name became connected with FBI security checks, such as the Chambers-Hiss investigation of the late 1940s, or with the invitation list to the White House Festival of the Arts sponsored by the Johnson administration in the mid-1960s. Five organizations and/or events that triggered FBI investigations during these three decades cover most of Trilling's dossier: the Trotsky Committee in 1937–38, the Revolutionary Workers League in 1944, the Hiss-Chambers saga during 1949–50, the Authors League of America in 1950–51, and the Festival of the Arts in 1965.

One might have expected Trilling's FBI dossier to have begun in 1932 or 1933, when he was a member of the NCDPP and an active fellow traveler whose allegiance was to revolutionary Marxism.[6] Trilling was a CP sympathizer long before his involvement with this communist-front organization; Mark Krupnick estimates that Trilling's embrace of revolutionary Marxist doctrine and radical activism "lasted about four years," ending at the time of the Moscow show trials in 1936–37.[7] If so, that would mean that FBI surveillance of him commenced just as his formal adherence to Marxism was concluding (though he apparently remained sympathetic to Marxism for a while longer).[8] After this time, however, Trilling did join the nonpartisan

Labor Defense, an independent radical group of anti-Stalinists. Trilling's literary activities during these years included politically aware book reviews (for example, for the *Nation* and *New Republic*); a socially sensitive Great Depression prose fiction work quite skeptical toward American bourgeois capitalist values (never completed and published in 2008 as *The Journey Abandoned*); and a dissertation on Matthew Arnold as man of letters and representative Victorian (published to acclaim in 1939).[9]

The FBI apparently opened a file on Trilling in February 1937 because he aroused the attention of the Bureau's New York office, which had launched an investigation of the members of the so-called Trotsky Committee, formally known as the American Committee for the Defense of Leon Trotsky, which sponsored an inquiry into the charges against Trotsky during the Moscow Trials. The committee consisted of nationally prominent liberals and radicals, including John Dewey, Norman Thomas, Max Eastman, Suzanne La Follette, and James Farrell. Other members belonged to Trilling's immediate circle around *Partisan Review*—Meyer Schapiro, Edmund Wilson, Mary McCarthy, James Rorty, and Sidney Hook. The acting secretary was a good friend of Trilling's and a lifelong Trotskyist functionary and ideologist, George Novack.[10] Trilling's FBI file includes several letters from Novack to him and to the other Trotsky Committee members, and the FBI memos bear numerous underlinings and notations next to the names of Trotsky Committee members listed on the official committee letterhead.

Trilling may have supported the committee's activities financially as well as intellectually. A June 22, 1937, letter from Novack reported on the Mexican hearings conducted by John Dewey, which Harper and Brothers had agreed to publish "provided the Committee purchase 2,000 copies in advance. *We must act immediately, and to do so must have your aid.*" Trilling was asked to contribute to the fund established to publish the hearings. Unfortunately, the FBI file does not disclose Trilling's personal response to these requests from the committee, nor does it record whether he contributed much more than his name and reputation to its activities. A second memo, issued on October 18, 1944, by the Bureau's Chicago office reopened Trilling's file and addressed his loose affiliation with the runaway Trotskyist faction of the Workers Party, the Revolutionary Workers League (RWL), which split away in 1935 in opposition to the party's Popular Front policy.[11]

One special agent attended an RWL meeting in Chicago on October 9, 1943. His report, along with reports of other agents (on meetings of May 12 and August 1, 1944, in Cleveland and on September 6, 1944, in Chicago), were sent directly to FBI director J. Edgar Hoover's office. One meeting is described as follows: "The evening was devoted to a discussion of theoretical Marxism and some time was devoted to the drafting of a resolution with reference to the No Strike Pledge which apparently was to be introduced at the coming United Automobile Workers Convention in Grand Rapids, Michigan." The memo—which focused on Sid Okun, acting national secretary of the RWL— also included the names of the members and contacts of the RWL in various states. Trilling's address appears on this list of names to support activities defending a Michigan African American who was tried and executed for the murder of his white landlord. A lengthy FBI report dated October 8, 1944, and titled "Revolutionary Worker's League," includes references to Trilling. According to a memo of July 31, 1950, summaries of RWL activities based on articles from newspapers and magazines such as *Compass* were later added to Trilling's file.

THE CHAMBERS CONNECTION

The most substantial section of Trilling's FBI file, however, deals with his connection to Whittaker Chambers. This third section of Trilling's file begins in March 1949. On March 9, an FBI agent in New York sent Hoover's office a copy of *The Middle of the Journey*, along with a summary of an article that had appeared in the February 13 *New York Herald Tribune*. The summary discussed the parallels between Trilling's novel and the developing perjury case against Hiss that featured Chambers as the chief accuser for the prosecution.[12] The article by Bert Andrews was headlined "Novel Written in 1947 Parallels Much of the Hiss-Chambers Story."[13]

A special assistant to the attorney general, Thomas J. Donegan, read this article and asked for a copy of the novel to determine whether its information "could possibly be of use to Hiss and his attorneys." The FBI agent noted that "there was some question as to whether the book or the author would figure in the trial of Alger Hiss."[14] As Trilling recalled in his introduction to the 1975 edition of *The Middle of the Journey*, he had refused in 1949 to appear before the House Un-American Activities Committee to testify about Chambers, characterizing him as a "man of honor."[15] However, the agent concluded, "This book has been reviewed and it is not believed that any information contained in this book is of any value in this investigation, although there is some similarity to Chambers' activities after he had broken from the Communist Party in 1938. This was explained by Mr. Trilling in his statements [during a 1949 FBI interview] that he had known Chambers and that portions of his book were written on the basis of his knowledge of Chambers' background."[16] Two agents had interviewed Trilling in 1949 about the novel, but his file contains no details about the interview.

The New York office then sent a full-length report, compiled by Special Agent Thomas G. Spencer and dated May 11, 1949, to Hoover. The memoranda included extensive written statements submitted by Chambers. The purpose of the report was to show "the connection between certain unknown subjects and activities mentioned by Chambers, and those mentioned by other informants. . . . A review of the information . . . has indicated beyond any doubt that they were members of the same Soviet espionage group." Copies of this memorandum were also submitted to a number of FBI regional bureaus, including the offices in Boston, Baltimore, Denver, Los Angeles, New Haven, Philadelphia, San Francisco, and Washington, D.C.

Later, under the section "Leads," Spencer, a New York agent, promises to interview Trilling again for information regarding Chambers. Spencer did so on October 12, 1950, at which time Trilling reported that he and Chambers had never visited in each other's homes; nevertheless, Trilling said, he "feels that he is very well acquainted with Chambers." Trilling described Chambers as "possessing a strong sense of social decency" and that he had an "extremely gentle, kind manner." But Trilling knew "very little" concerning other members of Chambers's circle.

Most of the material in this section of Trilling's file does not pertain directly to him or to *The Middle of the Journey*. The comprehensive May 1949 FBI report chiefly covers Chambers's activities from 1934 to 1938, when he was a member of the Communist Party and the CP underground. Several agents from the New York and Baltimore offices compiled Chambers's "Personal History" based on interviews with Chambers by special agents J. J. Ward, F. X. Plant, and Thomas G. Spencer. It begins in classical fashion: "I was born in Philadelphia, Pennsylvania on 1 April 1901 as J. Vivian Chambers."[17] Several pages then follow about Chambers's childhood and rearing. The level of detail extends to mentioning that "the attending physician [at Chambers' birth] was a Dr. Dunning."

FBI agents carefully indexed Chambers's statement. The section dealing with his college years at Columbia, when he served as editor of *Columbia Magazine*, includes scattered mentions of Trilling's name with the surrounding contents blacked out.[18] Also appearing in the Chambers section of Trilling's file is a summary of a hostile November 24, 1947, *Daily Worker* review of *The Middle of the Journey* by Ben Levine. Another review, written by Frank C. Hanighen and dated April 4, 1949, is also included in Trilling's file and had appeared in *Not Merely Gossip*, a supplement to *Human Events*, a right-wing magazine that soon became a supporter of Joseph McCarthy.

That article, "Spies," says that within intellectual circles, there was "a revived interest in a half-forgotten volume reputed to contain the answer to a

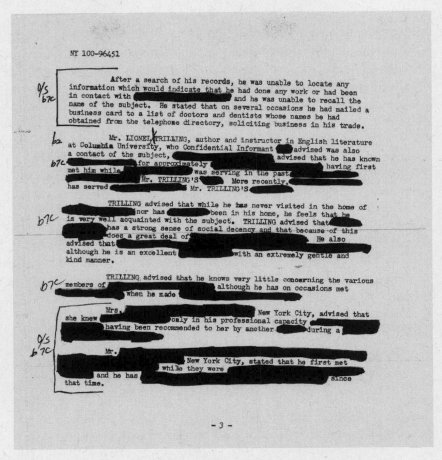

After a search of his records, he was unable to locate any information which would indicate that he had done any work or had been in contact with ████████ and he was unable to recall the name of the subject. He stated that on several occasions he had mailed a business card to a list of doctors and dentists whose names he had obtained from the telephone directory, soliciting business in his trade.

Mr. LIONEL TRILLING, author and instructor in English literature at Columbia University, who Confidential Informant ████ advised was also a contact of the subject, ████████ advised that he has known ████████ for approximately ████████ having first met him while ████████ was serving in the past ████████ has served ████████ Mr. TRILLING'S ████████ More recently, ████████ Mr. TRILLING'S ████████

TRILLING advised that while he has never visited in the home of ████████ nor has ████████ been in his home, he feels that he is very well acquainted with the subject. TRILLING advised that ████████ has a strong sense of social decency and that because of this ████████ does a great deal of ████████ He also advised that ████████ although he is an excellent ████████ with an extremely gentle and kind manner.

TRILLING advised that he knows very little concerning the various members of ████████ although he has on occasions met ████████ when he made ████████

Mrs. ████████ New York City, advised that she knew ████████ only in his professional capacity ████████ having been recommended to her by another ████████ during a ████████

Mr. ████████ New York City, stated that he first met ████████ while they were ████████ and he has ████████ since that time.

– 3 –

This FBI document is from the section of Trilling's file that pertains to his relationship with Whittaker Chambers. Despite the tenuous connection between the two—Trilling had partly based one of his characters in *The Middle of the Journey* (1947) on Chambers—dozens of pages about Chambers appear in Trilling's dossier.

key problem to the current espionage *cause célèbre*. The book is *The Middle of the Journey*, a novel by the distinguished literary critic Lionel Trilling and it was published in 1947, a year and a half before Mr. Chambers made his appearance on the public proscenium."[19] The agent adds, "If the author did not know something about at least one of the now widely publicized persons, he must have had clairvoyant imagination." The Hanighen review also cites a few parallels between Trilling's novel and Chambers's character and history.

THE AUTHORS LEAGUE OF (UN)AMERICA?

A fourth and related issue that renewed the FBI's interest in Trilling involved the Authors League of America, on whose board Trilling also served. Founded in 1912, the Authors League represents the interests of authors and playwrights regarding copyright, freedom of expression, taxation, and other issues. Consisting of two component organizations, the Dramatists Guild and the Authors Guild, it is the national society of professional authors and today represents more than sixty-five hundred writers of books, poetry, articles, short stories, and other literary works pertaining both to business and professional matters.

The Authors League came to the attention of the FBI because Chambers, in his capacity as a *Time* editor, contended in his statement to the FBI that John Hersey, chief of the magazine's Moscow bureau in the early 1940s, submitted reports for *Time* that were "obviously and quite openly quite favorable to the Union of [Soviet] Socialist Republics." (Hersey was vice president of the Authors League under President Oscar Hammerstein; Eric Barnouw served as secretary; among the other officers were Lillian Hellman, Rex Stout, and Lionel Trilling.)

The legal justification for an FBI file to be opened on the Authors League and its members was the new, more vigorous enforcement in 1948 of the Smith Act, which permitted scrutiny for national security reasons of all members of "basic revolutionary groups" in any way connected to "the violent overthrow" of the U.S. government. Formally known as the Alien Registration Act of 1940, the Smith Act made it illegal to teach or advocate the overthrow of the government by force or violence. Adopted in 1940, it was first used against American leftists in 1943, when leaders in the Socialist Workers Party and their supporters in the Minneapolis Teamsters Union were convicted of engaging in seditious activities and sentenced to as much as sixteen months in jail.[20]

In addition to Chambers's testimony about Hersey, the Authors League attracted the FBI's notice because it outspokenly defended its members' civil liberties. In May 1950, the Authors League declared that the Supreme Court's refusal to review the case of the Hollywood Ten had perpetuated the situation in which there existed in the United States "a form of censorship dangerous to the rights and economic existence of all authors."[21] An FBI memo advised the Bureau's agents, "You are instructed to immediately institute a discreet investigation of the Authors League of America to determine whether there is any communist infiltration, influence or control in the League and the extent thereof. In view of the nature of this crime, the investigation must be most discreet."

But if the FBI's information gathering about other Authors League members was as slipshod as its investigation of Trilling, the Bureau's discretion certainly came at the cost of accuracy. For example, a memo from the New York office dated June 9, 1950, notes that Trilling "was listed as an instructor in the Institute for Social Research in 1941. He is also an English professor at Columbia University, and is the author of the novel entitled *The Middle of the Journey* and a number of book reviews from the *New York Times Book Review* section." The reference to the Institute for Social Research—the famous émigré Frankfurt School research group housed at Columbia during the 1930s and 1940s, which had included Max Horkheimer and Theodor Adorno, among others—is an excellent example of how an obvious error in data collection becomes enshrined in print in a secret file and thus gains the status of biographical fact. Trilling never had anything remotely to do with the Frankfurt School, though he may well have met a few of its members, especially Erich Fromm, who was closely acquainted with Trilling's intellectual associates around *Partisan Review* (such as Irving Howe) and who joined *Dissent*'s editorial board in the mid-1950s.

A memo of December 29, 1950, from the FBI's New York office closes the section of Trilling's file covering the Authors League. It underlines the Bureau's preoccupation with subversive communist organizations as the Red Scare began to build. The memo also notes that the New York membership of the Authors League was estimated at between three thousand and four thousand. "It is an independent organization operating as a labor union. . . . Information shows some of its members to be affiliated with the CP or communist front organizations, [whose members are] in the minority."

NO SECOND VISIT TO CAMELOT

Several regional offices intermittently followed Trilling's activities from the late 1950s to the mid-1960s. But he was no longer considered relevant to any pressing public issue of national security after the Red Scare and McCarthyism had subsided in the mid-1950s, and little new information appears in his dossier in this last decade.[22]

Nonetheless, Trilling's name also turns up in connection with counterintelligence programs against Fidel Castro and against Soviet anti-Semitic policies.[23] In the latter case, a pamphlet, *Is Anti-Semitism a Policy of the Present Soviet Government?*, was submitted to Hoover, along with a letter to the *New York Times* cosigned by seven individuals, including members of Trilling's circle of *Partisan Review* and Columbia University acquaintances such as Saul Bellow, Leslie Fiedler, Irving Howe, Alfred Kazin, Phillip Rahv, and Robert Penn Warren. The lengthy letter, "Soviet Treatment of Jews," described Soviet attempts to liquidate Jewish culture during the previous decade. It also asked that Soviet Jews be given the freedom to immigrate, noting that Israel had indicated a readiness to receive them.[24]

The New York office investigated Trilling between December 9, 1958, and January 22, 1959, and inquired into conversations between Trilling and the New York District Attorney's Office. The Trillings were carefully tracked during that six-week period. According to one confidential memo, on December 23, "Agents of the New York office observed the subject leave his residence at 8:20 a.m. He proceeded via taxi to Grand Central Station where they boarded a train at Track 37, scheduled to leave for Detroit, Michigan, 9 AM." Indeed, the report reads as if Trilling were being tailed, though the justification for such security—let alone the waste of U.S. taxpayers' money—is never made explicit in the file. We are merely informed that such measures are evidently preliminary to an updated security clearance for Trilling.[25]

The final major item in the Trilling dossier is another FBI security check, conducted at the request of the White House when Trilling was screened for a possible invitation from President Lyndon Johnson to attend the gala cultural event of his presidency, the White House Festival of the Arts. Unlike Dwight Macdonald, who later published a report of his visit, Trilling ultimately was not invited to Johnson's festival. One factor that may have played a role in Trilling's exclusion was that he and Diana were guests at the Kennedy White House in 1962 and received lavish praise from the president: Diana Trilling later recalled in her memoir, "A Visit to Camelot," that Kennedy had even exhibited an awareness of her husband's literary-critical studies, such as *The Liberal Imagination*.[26] Johnson harbored an intense dislike for Camelot admirers and an even greater aversion to those whom JFK admired.

The Johnson festival was scheduled for June 14, 1965, just as U.S. involvement in the Vietnam War was escalating dramatically. Prominent writers and intellectuals in Trilling's circle were being closely checked by U.S. government intelligence agencies and by the Johnson administration to ascertain whether their attendance would prove embarrassing to the president.[27] (Some background checks were obviously slipshod. As we shall see in chapter 3, always a loose cannon, Macdonald circulated a protest petition at the event that garnered fifty signatures, a quarter of guests in attendance.)[28]

Here again, Trilling's past connections with radical organizations turn up, and it is unclear whether they proved a cause for concern. The FBI's memo dated February 2, 1965, reiterated that its files "reveal that the name Lionel Trilling was carried on the 1937 letterhead for the American Committee for the Defense of Leon Trotsky." The Bureau report also noted again that the issue of the *Daily Worker* dated November 24, 1947, contained a review of

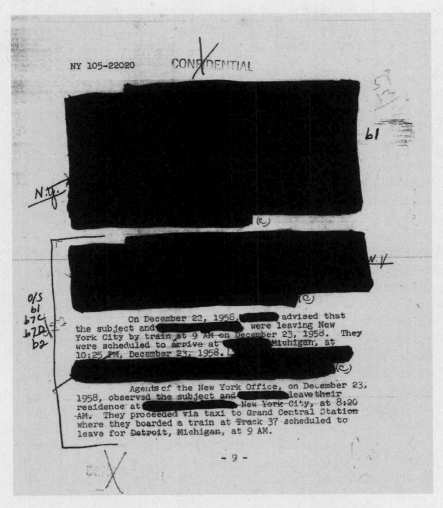

On December 22, 1958, [redacted] advised that the subject and [redacted] were leaving New York City by train at 9 AM on December 23, 1958. They were scheduled to arrive at [redacted] Michigan, at 10:25 PM, December 23, 1958.

Agents of the New York Office, on December 23, 1958, observed the subject and [redacted] leave their residence at [redacted] New York City, at 8:20 AM. They proceeded via taxi to Grand Central Station where they boarded a train at Track 37 scheduled to leave for Detroit, Michigan, at 9 AM.

- 9 -

Lionel and Diana Trilling were tailed in December 1958 as they departed from their home and "proceeded via taxi to Grand Central Station where they boarded a train at Track 37 scheduled to leave for Detroit, Michigan, at 9 AM." Probably the Trillings were making a Christmas visit during the winter break at Columbia University to friends or colleagues in Detroit. The file contains no explanation of why their movements were tracked; it also is not apparent why this document would need to be so heavily redacted when I received it several decades after the event.

The Middle of the Journey that characterized it "as a vicious novel and as being cold, calculated slander of the Communist Party. It was also stated that the book was designed to give the reader one single impression—that the Communist Party in the U.S. is an innocent front for another sinister force."

UNWANTED BY THE FBI:
TRILLING THE NON-COMMUNIST

Trilling's FBI dossier contains no bombshell revelations and discloses no technical violations of his civil liberties. But that does not lessen its interest or its representative significance on a number of grounds. First, the total number of pages in Trilling's dossier shows the thoroughness—or obsessiveness—with which the Bureau cataloged even the most trivial references to a subject. Presumably, files also exist under the names of other members of the American Committee for the Defense of Leon Trotsky, or other members on the RWL mailing list, or all those names mentioned in connection with the Alger Hiss–Whittaker Chambers case. When one considers that no formal field investigation of Trilling was ever conducted, the frequency with which his name surfaces in FBI records is noteworthy. (The same holds true for Alfred Kazin.)[29]

Second, a fact most surprising to several scholars at the 2005 Lionel Trilling Centennial Symposium in Louisiana, most of whom were unfamiliar with the research methods of intelligence agencies, was that these extensive FBI files make no reference to any of his numerous nonfiction works, such as *Matthew Arnold* (1939) or *The Liberal Imagination*, which received glowing reviews across America in 1950–51, or to any of the quasi-political articles that he wrote for pro-Stalinist publications of the 1930s such as the *Nation* and the *New Republic*.

As I had discovered decades earlier in my examination of several intelligence agency dossiers of George Orwell, G-men are not readers. They are listeners and sometimes interviewers. But they do not bother much with the kinds of literary research that most scholars conduct. The only title that agents ever even cite in Trilling's file is his novel, *The Middle of the Journey*, obviously because of its relevance to the Hiss-Chambers case. (Trilling's application of his knowledge about communism toward literary ends also did not arouse any interest from the FBI.)[30] Oddly, the file does not allude at any point to the NCDDP, the Communist-front organization that he joined (though it is conceivable that references are made to it in some of the pages blacked out in the dossier). Rather, the file indicates that FBI agents are not inclined to read and instead simply rely on newspaper accounts and the tips of informants. Indeed the Bureau's entire investigative approach to Trilling and his literary acquaintances stands as an ironic commentary on Nathan Zuckerman's line in Philip Roth's *The Prague Orgy*: "The police are like literary critics—of what little they see, they get most wrong anyway."[31] Amusingly, as Trilling's FBI dossier shows, in America—despite assembling comparable mountains of surveillance data—the "intelligence" agents are the *non*literary critics (i.e., they cannot be bothered to read texts).

Third, several Trilling scholars at the symposium in 2005 were surprised to learn that the Bureau investigated Trilling extensively even though he had become—as their own report on *The Middle of the Journey* recognized—a firm *anti*-Stalinist. But the FBI was not very keen on distinctions within left-wing circles. Agents could not understand splits between Trotskyists and Stalinists and were suspicious, always looking for conspiracies.

This fact brings to mind a hilarious (perhaps apocryphal?) story that Alfred Kazin told me. He said that it circulated widely about the intelligence-gathering agencies as well as the local police in the mid-1930s. A memorial was being held in 1934 in New York's old Madison Square Garden to honor the Austrian Socialists who had risen up against Dollfuss's fascist regime and were slaughtered with Mussolini's assistance. The memorial was broken up by Communist Party supporters loyal to Stalin who began throwing chairs down on participants from the upper balconies. People ran screaming out of the Garden, and a minor riot broke out between the two rival groups, attracting a number of curious onlookers. Within moments, the police and some G-men were on the scene, dragging people away and banging a few heads. One man being hauled off was heard to protest to a burly New York cop, "But Officer, I'm an *anti*-communist!!" The gruff reply came with a firm tug: "Look! I don't care what kind of communist you are! You're coming down to the station!"[32]

All this also points to a larger irony.[33] During the period when he was under FBI surveillance in the early post-war era, Trilling became quite approving of American political and cultural life as reflected in *Partisan Review*'s famous 1952 symposium, "Our Country and Our Culture," when he applauded "the great American tradition of non-conformism," lauding the "American way of life" for its "pluralism" and "diversity."[34] Irving Howe, Delmore Schwartz, and Joseph Frank criticized Trilling during the 1950s for his allegedly uncritical celebration of American culture and his "complacency" and "accommodations" toward U.S. shortcomings.[35] In light of his FBI file, their criticisms possess greater force than Trilling's conservative admirers have allowed.

But the additional irony points back to the Bureau itself, which, as Kazin's anecdote shows, remained utterly incapable of understanding American intellectual culture and its relationship to public life. The FBI never seems to have figured out which American intellectuals presented security risks, as is evidenced by the contrasting treatments of Trilling and Macdonald. It was common knowledge in New York that Macdonald was always a mercurial spirit and more willing than Trilling to take chances (the 1965 Festival of the Arts petition, the 1968 Columbia student strike, and so forth). Yet Macdonald was given a pass by the Bureau and thus permitted to embarrass Johnson at the Festival of the Arts. (Critics of the Bush administration's Patriot Act would maintain that intellectuals' experience at the hands of the American "intelligence" agencies is no different today.)

Fourth, Trilling's FBI dossier possesses representative significance as an illustration of the kinds of subjects that occupied intellectuals of the 1930s and 1940s and of the types of organizations and activities of intellectuals that American intelligence-gathering agencies investigated during those decades. Trilling himself was certainly no security threat. Yet because of his youthful affiliation with a communist organization and his personal acquaintance with Chambers—and particularly because Chambers featured as a central protagonist in *The Middle of the Journey*—Trilling drew the attention of the FBI and other intelligence organizations. The timing of *The Middle of the Journey*'s publication in 1947, just months before the Hiss-Chambers case exploded in the press, probably played a decisive role in renewing the FBI's interest in Trilling.[36] The novel obviously resulted in an enormous expansion of his FBI dossier. If it were not for his early communist flirtation and later his treatment of Chambers in his novel, it is highly unlikely that the FBI would have paid any sustained attention to him at all. Far more than most other members of the *Partisan Review* group—above all, far more than either Macdonald or Howe—Trilling's active involvement with communism was minimal and lay roughly fifteen years in his past by the time of the Hiss-Chambers case. Still, given the ignorance of intelligence agents about the history of American radicalism and the activities of many American intellectuals, Trilling's one-time affiliation with a communist-front organization forever marked him as a potential risk in the eyes of some FBI agents. That is to say, as is indicated by the renewal in the 1950s of the FBI's pre-war interest in the activities of radical American intellectuals, "You can never outrun your history." Or, as the Kazin anecdote suggests, "Once a communist, always a communist."

If so, then the past is never truly passed. From this point of view, as I mention in the Introduction, Trilling's FBI dossier traces the shadow life,

Lionel Trilling in his sixties in front of Columbia University's Butler Library.
Courtesy: University Archives, Columbia University

as it were, of Trilling's progressive (or "subversive") connections with communism beyond his formal association with Communists and their activities in the early 1930s. The dossier may therefore also be viewed as a penumbra of his past, demonstrating how the past lives on into the present—and in fact the files do furnish a shadowy reflection of his ongoing, if limited and tangential, connections to various students, colleagues, and acquaintances still affiliated with communist groups and activities long after Trilling had dissociated himself formally from any such organizational relationship.[37]

Trilling, like many others of his generation, was on the fringe of various left-wing movements, a position that brought him into contact with the FBI. He had a minor involvement with the Trotsky Committee but very little contact thereafter with communist circles. (One scholar has recently examined Trilling's activities and writings in close detail during the early 1930s and has characterized this period of Trilling's life, "Trilling the Communist."[38] But Trilling's FBI dossier suggests that his entire career after the age of thirty should instead properly be characterized as "Trilling the Non-Communist.") Indeed Trilling's FBI file also shows that he posed no security risk to Columbia University. That is doubtless why he was cleared in 1953, as McCarthyism and the so-called witch hunts in the American academy were still on the rise, to head the university's faculty committee that evaluated professors and staff members for national loyalty.

All this prompts another question: How might Trilling have reacted if *he* had obtained his FBI file and discovered that the Bureau had snooped on him? I doubt the Keystone Cops investigation into Trilling's life would have drastically changed his political views during the 1950s (or later) if he had known about it. I doubt that his pro-Americanism would have been much shaken. Trilling's parents were very pro-American (much more than were the parents of the other leading *PR* writers). Even in the mid-1930s, Trilling was not disgusted with America,[39] and his early post-war support for America had to do with weighty geopolitical matters: America as the wartime foe of Nazi Germany, America as the Cold War bulwark against the Soviet Union, America as the Western showcase of cultural and intellectual creativity. Trilling's sympathy with the "American Way of Life" had also to do with something more archaic as well—he believed that support for one's country was not a function of circumstance but rather a matter of honor, something that was almost Victorian in Trilling (and that he perceived in Orwell, for example). Trilling would have found his own FBI file silly and slightly sinister, but he likely would have dismissed it as a bizarre side effect of the Hiss case.[40]

So Trilling's treatment by the Bureau is not a case study in political repression. He certainly was no victim of McCarthyism—unlike the cases of the blacklisted Hollywood radicals and numerous famous literary figures on the Left.[41] During the 1968 Columbia riots, student radicals may have decried his anti-communism and put up posters bearing his picture with the inscription "Wanted, Dead or Alive, for Crimes against Humanity," but the G-men didn't really want him. They were never truly preoccupied with him—only with some of his acquaintances.

Nonetheless, the Trilling files offer a salutary lesson. Americans today must expect—and speak out against—even "mild" infringements on our civil liberties such as this one. Trilling was a leading American professor by the mid-1940s and had not been affiliated with any left-wing political organization for more than a decade; he was favored in the 1950s with government-sponsored and -financed junkets to Europe, courtesy of *Perspectives USA*, a CIA-front publication that fell loosely under the umbrella of the Congress for Cultural Freedom (whose CIA connection was not publicly exposed until the mid-1960s.[42] If anyone was politically safe as a U.S. government security risk by the mid-century, it was Lionel Trilling. At best, Trilling's surveillance by the FBI was wasteful and misguided. Our public servants owe the American citizenry both wiser decisions about the allocation of government resources and greater respect for our personal freedoms.

Dwight Macdonald in East Hampton, New York, 1979.
Courtesy: Nick Macdonald

CHAPTER THREE

FROM FBI NOSE-TWEAKER TO CIA "STOOGE" TO LBJ'S NEMESIS

DWIGHT MACDONALD, A "CRITICAL (UN?)AMERICAN"

CUM LAUDE ON THE "AMERICAN 'HONORS LIST'" OF SUBVERSIVES

If there was one thing that J. Edgar Hoover fiercely cherished, it was the reputation of the Federal Bureau of Investigation (FBI) as the incorruptible, all-powerful guardian of America from its nefarious enemies, both domestic and foreign. From 1924 to 1972, Director Hoover carefully sculpted his proudly held image of the honest G-man through a public relations campaign that portrayed the Bureau in a flattering light in books, magazine articles, newspaper reports, films, radio programs, and eventually television shows.[1]

From this sensitivity grew a tradition of trying to counter any individual or group that threatened what Hoover saw as the integrity of the agency that he had crafted into an Argus-eyed behemoth—indeed, into one of the most powerful national police forces in the world. As a result, innocuous though the threat might have seemed, it did not pass the Bureau's watchful gaze unnoticed when a little-known Trotskyist-anarchist-pacifist journalist had the audacity to scribble a few lines of defiant graffiti on Hoover's masterwork.

In 1942, puckishly defiant journalist Dwight Macdonald (1906–82) tweaked Hoover's nose in a fledgling, left-wing, New York little magazine and thereby ran afoul of Hoover's massive public relations machine. Because of Macdonald's activities on behalf of various radical causes and his writings in the quasi-Trotskyist intellectual quarterly *Partisan Review*—destined to become the leading literary journal of the post-war era yet still relatively unknown outside New York intellectual circles—FBI agents compiled a dossier on Macdonald in the spring of 1942. They tracked his life since 1929, noting the places he worked, the articles he wrote, and the political affiliations he established. Their fact gathering was spotty: for instance, they claimed that Macdonald (usually spelled "McDonald") was a registered Communist Party (CP) member in New York in 1937 and thereafter broke with the party. In fact, Macdonald was never a CP member; he despised the Stalinists, chafed at party discipline from commissars of all kinds, and was a consistent enemy of orthodox Soviet communism and its fellow travelers throughout his long career.

Dwight Macdonald was, however, a heterodox socialist and (as one FBI agent put it) "Trotzkyite." In September 1939, following the Nazi-Soviet pact in August and the subsequent invasion of Poland by the Germans and Russians, he joined the Socialist Workers Party (SWP), which had been formed from a Trotskyist group that had split off from the Socialist Party. During the previous year, after serving as a staff writer for Henry Luce's *Fortune* and contributing regularly to various Trotskyist magazines in the mid-1930s, Macdonald had joined the editorial board of *Partisan Review*, which at this time was sympathetic to Trotskyism. In 1943, Macdonald broke with his *PR* colleagues and in 1944 founded his own magazine, *politics* (which he always proudly lowercased). He had fallen out with editors Philip Rahv and William Phillips over support for the Allied war effort and on a variety of cultural matters. Macdonald wanted to express with unbridled freedom his own idiosyncratic anti-war views and hold forth on what he regarded as the lamentable state of American radicalism.[2]

The FBI began keeping tabs on Macdonald once he started raising money for *politics* from like-minded former (and current) Trotskyists and/or Socialist Workers Party members. Macdonald probably would have been pleased to know that he remained on the Bureau's checklist of political radicals for a quarter century. He would have agreed with E. L. Doctorow that an FBI dossier placed one "on an American 'honors list.'"[3] He might have been chagrined to learn, however, that he never rose to the august level of "security risk" (unlike his former assistant, Irving Howe, a onetime *politics* editorial board member and Trotskyist).[4]

The FBI's agents struggled vainly to make sense of where Macdonald fit in the broader picture of American dissent. They could never quite get a handle on him, though they pursued him for decades, to use Oscar Wilde's phrase, with "all the enthusiasm of a short-sighted detective."[5]

Macdonald's FBI file totals more than seven hundred pages—hundreds more than suspect writers (such as Ernest Hemingway or Dashiell Hammett) or other former Trotskyist intellectuals (such as Howe). Scrutiny of its contents not only furnishes a fascinating snapshot of what was happening in one corner of the Left in the middle decades of the twentieth century but also anatomizes how a uniquely gifted—and burdened—intellectual engaged with his times as the political landscape altered and his social and cultural convictions evolved.

Although the FBI's failure to comprehend the American radical scene led to a fundamental misunderstanding of Macdonald's politics (and *politics*), that alone does not fully account for the Bureau's confusions about him. The fact is that Macdonald was a gadfly and avowed outsider—and he was sui generis, as Czeslaw Miłosz noted.[6] Fundamental to his sometimes puzzling eclecticism and irrepressible distinctiveness—and an abiding source of his interest today—was his conservative ethos. For although Macdonald was invariably a left-wing anti-capitalist whose political stands zigzagged from Trotskyism to anarcho-pacifism to quietism to liberal anti-communism to born-again New Left radicalism, he was fundamentally a cultural conservative on aesthetic matters and a vocal highbrow defender of traditional cultural norms. Radical by conviction, Macdonald was conservative in temperament and taste, and this made him an unabashed champion of established classical standards and even a curmudgeonly elitist in his later years. He came to hate avant-garde art and lashed out at both the action painting of Jackson Pollock and Beat writers such as Allen Ginsberg and Jack Kerouac. Unlike most of his fellow intellectuals associated with *Partisan Review*, Macdonald supported awarding the Bollingen Prize for Poetry to Ezra Pound for his *Pisan Cantos* in 1948. A great admirer of sophisticated European modernism, Macdonald condemned the poetry for its anti-Semitism, but he praised the judging panel for having conferred the prize on the basis of literary quality, leaving aside all political considerations, including the fact that Pound was accused of treason for his participation in Italian fascist propaganda against the Allies during World War II. Macdonald noted approvingly that no such state-supported award honoring the autonomy of art could possibly be given in a fascist or communist country.

And yet for concerned citizens today, the ultimate significance of the FBI's misguided pursuit of Dwight Macdonald is not the stale joke that "U.S. intelligence" is a contradiction in terms, let alone that Macdonald is a forgotten literary burnout. Rather, it is that we Americans need to remain wary of official rationales for invading our privacy, which invariably invoke issues of "national security" or "patriotism" or even the "public good."

Equally notable in light of the Bureau's misconceptions about Macdonald is his freelance style—in life as well as in literature. For if ever there was an "individualist" whose eclectic career amounted to its own one-man, quixotic crusade, it was Dwight Macdonald. Czeslaw Miłosz once called him "a totally American phenomenon in the tradition of Thoreau, Whitman, and Melville—'the completely free man,' capable of making decisions at all times and about all things, strictly on the basis of his personal and moral judgment."[7] It is this Macdonald, the moralist and outsider, who speaks to so many libertarians of our time and yet also wins allegiance from cultural conservatives (Christopher Hitchens) and academic radicals (Alan Wald). His anti-statism, his anarchist impulse, his Veblerian distrust for the academy and its pretensions, his impassioned defense of cultural norms and the Western literary tradition: these capacities are indispensable field artillery in the ongoing culture wars of the twenty-first century. For all these reasons, Macdonald should still exert a claim on our interest and attention today.

DWIGHT MacDONALD, McDONALD, MACDONALD HAD A . . . JOURNAL

In the course of circulating fund-raising letters in late 1943 for *politics*, Macdonald caught the attention of the FBI, which opened another dossier on him and launched a fresh investigation into his activities. What especially piqued the FBI's interest was the correspondence between Macdonald and a potential contributor to the magazine, Victor Serge, whose real name was Kibalchich. The Bureau believed that Macdonald was trying to arrange for Serge to settle in the United States. Serge was an ex-Communist and prolific author whose rejection of Stalinist orthodoxies and fierce commitment to democratic socialism had rendered him persona non grata in the Soviet Union. Although the independent-minded Serge was a fearless critic of the Bolshevik state's claim to represent revolutionary socialism, the FBI regarded him as a dangerous subversive who should be kept out of the United States at all costs. He was living in Mexico when Macdonald contacted him about contributing an article to *politics*. The FBI was compiling a list of writers who represented national security threats, and Macdonald's name joined that growing number. Unlike the case of Irving Howe, however, a Security Index file was never formally opened on Macdonald.

The Bureau's probe of Macdonald's activities intensified in 1944 after he founded *politics*, which he almost singlehandedly published, edited, and even wrote during the next five years. With a bureaucratic mix of clumsiness and thoroughness, the Bureau carried out a background check on Macdonald—spelling his name incorrectly as *MacDonald* or *McDonald* even after he became an internationally recognized writer. They also began to monitor his mail; copies of Serge's letters to him can be found in Macdonald's dossier. Checking the magazine's office, the Bureau discovered to its surprise that *politics'* entire staff consisted of just three people: Macdonald; his wife, Nancy; and a secretary/assistant, Dorothy Frumm. The Bureau then launched an investigation of Frumm, finding nothing of significance.

The Macdonald file serves as an ironic commentary on the FBI of the mid-twentieth century, exposing yet another huge blind spot when it came to the Bureau's surveillance of the American Left. The Bureau tended to equate everyone on the left with communism, since few agents were familiar with the immigrant origins and European context of radical politics in America.[8] The FBI viewed anyone with a liberal or radical past as suspect for tolerating communists and defending their constitutional rights. The Macdonald file reflects little awareness of the sectarian battles that raged within the American Left. The lasting impression is of a sense of bewilderment on the part of various agents as they try to disentangle the complex connections among rival left-wing groups. Macdonald's dossier possesses significant historical and political value, offering a revealing glimpse of the vicissitudes of post-war U.S. intellectual life—seen from the veiled side of government intelligence documents—as the American Left lurched along in turmoil during World War II, through the Cold War, and into the era of the Vietnam War protests.

OR DWIGHT "McCARTHY"?

On January 26, 1944, J. Edgar Hoover ordered a full-scale investigation of Macdonald and his new journal. On April 6, the Albany branch of the FBI's New York office filed a report, "Dwight Macdonald alias McCarthy." The name McCarthy had already appeared occasionally in the FBI reports on Macdonald, indicating that their agents claimed he was a well-known Stalinist in Washington, D.C., in 1937. The FBI periodically would record the possibility that Macdonald was (to use the then-current phrase) "a card-carrying member of the Communist Party." The source for this misconception was an informant who had read (and misunderstood) Macdonald's magazine.

The FBI seldom took such regional office reports as the last word. Yet the very claim that Macdonald ("alias McCarthy") was a Washington, D.C., Stalinist operative in 1937 reflects the Bureau's confusion about American radical politics. In 1937, when Macdonald was supposed to be agitating for

Stalinism in the nation's capital, he was living in New York and embroiled in literary politics, devising strategies and tactics with his fellow Trotskyists for seizing *Partisan Review* from the Stalinists who had founded the magazine in 1934 and still controlled it. He was also involved that year with John Dewey's American Committee for the Defense of Leon Trotsky, which was challenging the accusations against Trotsky emerging from the Moscow purge trials—scarcely the activities one would associate with a Stalinist.

It is not apparent whether the FBI ever cleared up its New York/Washington, D.C., "Doppelgänger Dwight" identity confusions. Toward the end of Macdonald's file, which closes in the early 1970s, however, the references to him as a Communist dwindle. Nonetheless, the mix-up attests to the FBI's uncertain grasp of the nature of the wartime and post-war American Left.

The April 1944 report also includes an up-to-date thumbnail biography of Macdonald: his various residences, his financial status, the names of his wife and children, and a review of the first two issues of *politics*. Subsequent reports obtained from what the FBI called "confidential informants whose identity is known to the Bureau" dispute the contention that Macdonald was a Stalinist or Communist sympathizer. One informant told the FBI not only that Communist Party orthodoxy repelled Macdonald but also that he could not abide even the milder variant found among Trotskyist sects. He could not in fact stomach the shibboleths of Soviet ideology, especially after the start of the war in September 1939 and Trotsky's murder the following August. The informant stated that Macdonald "left the [Socialist] Workers Party in 1941 because he could not accept Bolshevism in its original form. He believed that Leninism as practiced in Russia had failed and believed a Socialist revolution unlikely but thought that new ways and means would have to be devised in order to accomplish it."[9]

Another instance of Macdonald's opposition to Stalin's Russia was gathered from FBI informants. They noted that he had been arrested for disorderly conduct on August 30, 1940, outside the Soviet consulate in New York, where he was protesting Stalin's alliance with Hitler.

Another "confidential informant" told the FBI that Macdonald was secretary of an organization including influential anti-Stalinist leftists (such as James T. Farrell, Sidney Hook, Norman Thomas, and Edmund Wilson) that was created to protest the pro-Soviet film *Mission to Moscow* (1943), a Hollywood drama designed to strengthen the wartime alliance with "Uncle Joe." Based on the memoirs of Joseph E. Davies, ambassador to Russia from 1937 to 1939, *Mission to Moscow* was a full-scale whitewash of Stalin's crimes and his purge trials. The film also rationalized the Nazi-Soviet pact as a step forced on Stalin by the West.[10] One would think Macdonald's anti-Soviet stance would have satisfied Hoover that *politics* represented no real threat to the nation's security. It also should have alerted the Bureau to the complexities of American intellectual radicalism and some of the distinctions between the anti-Stalinist Left and the Stalinist Left at this time.

But it did not. The Bureau's agents stayed on Macdonald's case. They even took out a subscription to *politics* "through a confidential mail box maintained by the New York office." Macdonald would probably have been gratified to learn that the Bureau was a paid subscriber, given that *politics* struggled throughout its five-year history and never gained more than five thousand subscribers.[11]

The FBI's assiduous monitoring of the wartime *politics* unearthed no juicy scandals or bombshell revelations. Much of the magazine's anarchist-pacifist, anti-capitalist, and anti–New Deal editorial line seemed unexceptional to FBI agents. Still, the FBI was puzzled by Macdonald's left-wing anti-communism, especially when the USSR was a valued ally during the war years. FBI agents continued to deliver periodic reports of *politics*' contents, all of which they forwarded to the main office in Washington. Hoover found nothing much of interest.

HOOVER'S "GESTAPO IN KNEE-PANTS"

That all changed in the post-war years. Macdonald commissioned an article in 1947 on Hoover and the FBI by a freelance writer, Clifton Northbridge Bennett, a self-declared anarchist and pacifist. Hoover was thin-skinned about even discreet private criticism, let alone any public castigation of the Bureau; he made strenuous efforts (with considerable success) through his public relations machine to ensure that only positive stories appeared.

By the early post-war era, Hoover's close working relationship with leading Washington politicians of both parties and with the nation's print barons and broadcast media newsmen guaranteed a constant stream of positive propaganda about his intrepid G-men. Their job was made easy because Hoover also had enjoyed "a good war." To glamorize the FBI's roundup of Nazis or pro-Nazi sympathizers in the United States, Hollywood added to Hoover's aura with *The House on 92nd Street* (1945), a highly successful film about the breakup of a Nazi espionage gang in New York. Hoover was so pleased by the film that he entered into a deal with Darryl Zanuck of Twentieth Century–Fox studios to make a film every year based on FBI cases. The two men soon clashed, however, and the project fell through.[12]

So the last thing Hoover wanted was for some muckraking, fellow-traveling Commie editor with a Leninist (or Trotskyite?) goatee and his hireling hack writer to dig up dirt on the director and his beloved Bureau—and then to publish it in their un-American scandal sheet. Macdonald and Bennett, however, were not intimidated by the FBI's reputation or cowed by Hoover's publicity machine. In April 1947, Bennett wrote to Hoover requesting an interview for his forthcoming article. Hoover was suspicious, refused to grant the interview, and then ordered that Bennett be investigated. The ensuing inquiry riveted the FBI's attention on *politics* once more.

The Bureau report on Bennett uncovered that he had been arrested by the FBI in 1945 for draft dodging and spent more than a year in jail before being released in December 1946. The report also asserted that Bennett was officially connected to *politics*, though FBI agents were not yet certain just how. In fact, he was writing his exposé of the Bureau as a freelancer. The report also noted that Bennett toured the FBI facility in Washington in 1947 and subsequently asked to meet with an FBI agent. At the meeting he asked a number of searching, uncomfortable questions that aroused the suspicions of the agent, who immediately drew up a report and sent it to Hoover.[13]

How Hoover dealt with unfavorable publicity can be gauged from the fact that the FBI thereupon contacted Bennett's parole board to see if there was any evidence to recommit him to prison. The parole board rejected that step on the grounds "that persons of Bennett's type would welcome this type of action and would therefore consider themselves martyrs."[14] The New York office told Hoover that Bennett's research agenda was to write "another smear attack against the Director."[15] Even gossip columnist Walter Winchell, then at the height of his popularity and quite cozy with Hoover, entered the fray. He got wind of Bennett's article and had his secretary forward a copy to Hoover, receiving a "Dear Walter" letter of thanks from the director in return.[16]

Hoover's ire was now aroused. In a memo written in late 1947 or early 1948, Hoover ordered Bureau agents to "keep an eye on MacDonald [*sic*] and his publication. He must have resources to put this out. He could easily be used by Commies even though he may claim to be pacifist." The FBI also checked the funding of *politics* to determine if any Stalinist front organizations were financing the journal.[17]

Hoover was apparently convinced that *politics* was a Stalinist front, a complete misreading of Macdonald and his magazine. Why the Bureau thought that Stalinists would back Macdonald—at a moment when *politics* was publishing a series of bitter assaults on Stalin's Soviet Union—is mystifying. Did they deem the series a clever ruse, an instance of Stalinist machinations, or an attempt at a disinformation campaign? Or was it another mini version of a nascent Popular Front strategy that would unite Stalinists with anarchist-pacifist intellectuals? Macdonald's dossier furnishes no clear answer.

Shortly after the Communist coup in Czechoslovakia in February 1948, Macdonald adopted an even harsher anti-Soviet line. He began castigating

Henry Wallace, the Progressive Party presidential candidate, as a Stalinist dupe. Some of Macdonald's *politics* columns on Wallace appeared in *Henry Wallace: The Man and the Myth* (1948), a fierce polemic that dismissed Wallace and his supporters as Stalinist hacks. Evidence of Macdonald's vociferous anti-communism and anti-Stalinism occasionally emerges in the FBI reports but never registered with Hoover, especially after Bennett's article appeared in the Winter 1948 issue of *politics*. It represents a classic case of how out of touch the FBI was with the post-war left-wing scene in America.

Bennett's article, "The F.B.I.," is a sustained critique of the Bureau. Written in plain prose, it traces the full development of the FBI under Hoover's leadership since the 1920s. Bennett implies that Hoover built his reputation falsely, even noting that his law degree was conferred without a written thesis. Bennett also points out that many of Hoover's articles and books, which Bennett describes as "lurid, alarmist, and imaginative with regard to fact," were ghosted by a professional writer, Courtney Ryley Cooper. Here especially, Bennett hit a raw nerve with the publicity-conscious Hoover.[18]

If that weren't enough to rankle Hoover, a section of Bennett's article bore the title "Gestapo in Knee-Pants." Comparing the FBI to the Gestapo made Hoover apoplectic. Bennett also cast doubt on two of Hoover's proudest accomplishments. First, Bennett claimed that Hoover had exaggerated his role in the arrest of Louis "Lepke" Buchalter, the head of Murder Inc. Second, Bennett contended that the Nazi saboteurs who landed in New York had not been hunted down by an FBI dragnet but rather had simply been betrayed by one of their own. Hoover was incensed. But he granted that he could not do much about *politics*—and he did not need to do much. Short of funds, *politics* was appearing sporadically; with its circulation declining, it was near collapse.

THE 1950S: "WHO IS HE?"

Shortly after the appearance of Bennett's piece, the FBI's New York office informed Hoover that Macdonald was planning to close down the magazine in early 1949. After this report, Macdonald dropped off the FBI's radar screen. He had in any case become disillusioned with the political scene and was now preoccupied with the world of culture, where he would channel his iconoclastic energies throughout the next decade, supported by his well-paid position as a freelance writer with the *New Yorker*.

Although his name would occasionally surface on one of the FBI's periodic investigations of American left-wing movements in the 1950s, the FBI lost interest in Macdonald during these years: he was not on any FBI watch list or its Security Index. Nonetheless, he still surfaced occasionally in FBI reports as a "Communist" or Communist Party member, as the FBI reports failed again and again to sort out intelligibly the plethora of leftist factions, wings, and sects. One frustrated agent wrote to Hoover that conducting interviews with members of the Socialist Workers Party and other Trotskyist groups was difficult because they "tend toward argument," an understatement that Macdonald would likely have affirmed with his trademark response on hearing such ingenuous obtuseness: a loud and long guffaw.[19]

Throughout the 1950s, the FBI collected Macdonald's articles from both the *New Yorker* and the London-based *Encounter*, for which he wrote occasional pieces. But agents found little that interested them. Hoover had forgotten him. In an April 1958 letter to the FBI's New York office about a negative *New York Times* review of his latest book, *Masters of Deceit*, Hoover noted that "Dwight Macdonald" was mentioned in passing in the review. "Who is he?" queried the director.[20] So much for the impression that *politics* and Macdonald had made on the FBI a decade earlier.

The biting review of Hoover's book in the *New York Times*, with its reference to Macdonald, triggered yet another investigation of "subversive" intellectuals. The FBI gathered up its old dossiers on Macdonald, but the only new information entered into his file concerns his role in protesting the pro-Soviet Conference on World Peace in March 1949—generally known as the Waldorf Conference, because it occurred at New York's Waldorf-Astoria Hotel. In its report the FBI describes Macdonald as a well-known "anti-Communist" and notes that his questions from the floor "attempted to turn the Conference into an anti-Soviet inquisition."[21]

Macdonald's name crops up periodically in FBI reports of the 1950s, primarily when he traveled abroad. For example, in the mid- and late 1950s, the Bureau tracked his trips to England and Argentina, though, here again, the FBI agents discovered little of interest. Hoover must have been aware that the Central Intelligence Agency (CIA) was monitoring Macdonald's activities (and soon putting him on its payroll—albeit without Macdonald's knowledge—as an editor of the FBI-subsidized *Encounter*). Macdonald's name also turns up in connection with the campaign to secure clemency for Morton Sobell, who was convicted in the Rosenberg spy case. But Macdonald was a peripheral figure, and Hoover was no longer concerned about him.[22]

MY COUNTRY, DWIGHT OR LEFT

Even as the FBI lost interest in Macdonald, his activities abroad were arousing the interest of the CIA and the State Department, precisely because of the negotiations that *Encounter* had commenced with him to become the associate editor of the magazine, replacing the staunchly pro-American Irving Kristol. *Encounter*, a London-based magazine supported by an American foundation and affiliated with the anti-Soviet Congress for Cultural Freedom (CCF), was a special project in the CIA's cultural campaign to promote the superiority of Western civilization over Sino-Soviet communism. The agency was secretly funding the magazine as part of its clandestine "Free World" outreach program to Europe under the auspices of its Paris-based front organization, the CCF. Macdonald occasionally contributed to the magazine, as did many other members of the *PR* circle.

Yet it was something completely different for him to be working in London as the American editor of *Encounter*, where he would presumably have regular contact with members of the British Committee of the Congress for Cultural Freedom and visit on a regular basis the CCF's Paris headquarters. He would inevitably learn all about the magazine's background and funding. This did not so much concern the CCF's executive director, Michael Josselson, who simply assumed that Macdonald was cut from the same cloth as most of the members of the American Committee for Cultural Freedom (ACCF), such as Kristol, Diana Trilling, Sidney Hook, and others. But ACCF members were alarmed and aghast. Josselson was surprised and dismayed to discover that Kristol and Hook, along with a majority of the other members of the ACCF, strongly objected to Macdonald receiving the nod as Kristol's replacement. Josselson had made a firm offer to Macdonald but soon backpedaled. Josselson tried to soften the rejection essentially by buying Macdonald off, appealing to his sense of adventure and his distaste for a conventional editorial desk job. Josselson's new gambit was simply to make Macdonald a contributor based in London, with no reduction in salary and even more freedom to travel.[23]

For practically anybody else, especially a working writer interested in promoting his own career by establishing his credentials on the international scene, this change would have been very welcome news. But Dwight Macdonald immediately perceived the snub and was outraged. Josselson was coming to understand that his friend Dwight was a congenital iconoclast whose reputation in New York was that of a mercurial gadfly. Yet Macdonald was also no fool, and after a few weeks of vituperative breast-beating, he calmed down and saw the benefit of Josselson's revised offer. Macdonald became an assistant editor and agreed to a one-year experiment during which he would serve as a kind of roving London-based correspondent.

Because Macdonald was traveling so much and enjoying his London activities and the new social world that it opened, his stay during 1956–57 was uncontroversial until shortly before his departure. What triggered the explosion, which worried voices on the ACCF had forecast and feared, was a Macdonald submission to *Encounter* that was rejected because it was deemed excessively critical of the United States. Macdonald later published it in another London-based magazine, *Twentieth Century*. But he fired off a proud, sharp letter to the editor of that periodical in December 1958, protesting the editorial introduction to "America! America!," Macdonald's essay that had appeared in the October issue. The editors of the British magazine had written that they "would not publish Dwight Macdonald's spirited and witty comment on American life" if Macdonald himself were not "a good American." Macdonald replied that "patriotism has never been my strong point." He continued, "I don't know as I'd call myself A Good American. I'm certainly A Critical American, and I prefer your country, morally and culturally, to my own."[24]

Macdonald had published his essay in *Twentieth Century* after *Encounter* had withdrawn its acceptance and rejected the piece. Macdonald suspected that *Encounter* had reversed itself on political grounds because his piece was sharply critical of Eisenhower-era America. Macdonald voiced his suspicions in a short *Dissent* essay published in the autumn of 1958. The issues were especially complicated because Macdonald had served as an editor of *Encounter* (1956–57) and because its editor-in-chief (who had accepted and then rejected "America! America!") was Kristol, a friendly acquaintance and fellow member of their New York intellectual circle. Kristol was indeed under political pressure from the CCF and its administrative secretary, Josselson. On first reading the *Dissent* piece, which also appeared in October in New York, an enraged Josselson wrote to John Hunt, a CCF staff member who was soon to be promoted to executive secretary of the international office of the CCF in Paris, that "America! America!" was "the most anti-American piece I have ever read and belongs in *Literaturnaya Gazeta*."[25]

Five months later, Josselson wrote from the CCF offices in Paris to Kristol about "Dwight's little introduction to his 'America! America!' in *Dissent*." Josselson ridiculed Macdonald's "two exhibitionist pieces about America that you and Stephen [Spender] were wrong in accepting in the first place. Dwight is mistaken if he thinks we were afraid of losing the support of some of the foundations if *Encounter* published his silly piece about America. I don't know how he ever got that idea."[26]

But Macdonald was right in his surmise about the "foundation" support generally and about the fate of his essay in particular. In 1967, news broke that the CCF and its magazines had been funded from the outset by the CIA. Later it became known that Josselson himself was on the CIA payroll.

Josselson, who remained on friendly terms with Macdonald despite all their political disagreements, wrote to him, "In the whole business there's nothing I'm ashamed of—except for the letter I wrote you about your *Encounter* piece on American life. My very next trip to the US showed me how much more you were in touch than I was. I am sorry to say I didn't apologize to you then and there."[27]

Indeed, when the revelations about the CIA's surreptitious funding of the CCF exploded in 1967, Macdonald professed to be shocked and outraged. He complained loudly to any available ear that he felt humiliated as "a CIA stooge."[28] Such wails of pained protest, however, simply confirmed the perceptions of his intellectual colleagues that he was a political buffoon, a jokester more in love with a good quip than with serious analysis.[29] To Irving Howe, Macdonald possessed a "table-hopping mind." Daniel Bell mocked him as "the floating kidney on the Left." Indeed, Macdonald could mothball intellectual fashions, but his own mercurial political enthusiasms rivaled the rise and fall of women's hemlines.[30]

Consistency never was Macdonald's strong suit. Yet it is also true that he was not taken seriously—especially by pure political types such as Hook and Rahv—because his sense of humor was unusual in the rarified atmosphere of the *Partisan Review* crowd, where comedy was considered something for the borscht belt. By the late 1940s he was in danger of being marginalized. His fellow *PR* editor, William Barrett, summarized the ultimate verdict of their intellectual community when he later wrote that for Macdonald, "every venture into politics was a leap toward the Absolute. . . . He was a kind of Don Quixote or Galahad, tilting at windmills in quest of the Holy Grail."[31]

THE 1960S: BACK TO THE BARRICADES

Another glancing blow at the windmill called Hoover—another bold leap to stomp on the director's photogenic public face—got under Hoover's skin and drew the Bureau back to Macdonald's case in the 1960s. This new act of Macdonald bravado exposed the gap between FBI publicity and reality. Once again, the circumstances highlight Hoover's sensitivity regarding his public image.

The occasion was Macdonald's slashing review in the March 1962 *Esquire* of a film sympathetic to the FBI, *Experiment in Terror*. Released by Columbia Pictures, directed by the highly regarded Blake Edwards, starring Glenn Ford and Lee Remick, and produced with the cooperation of the San Francisco FBI office, the film purported to show how the Bureau caught a bank robber and kidnapper. The film was a popular and critical hit. But Macdonald characteristically remained unimpressed. He found the film simplistic, nothing more than another exercise in Hollywood hagiography, a made-to-order product aiming to beatify the FBI. Reporting to Hoover on the *Esquire* review, FBI agents noted that Macdonald "does not like the movie. This is of no concern to us except that Macdonald uses the occasion to viciously criticize the FBI." One line from Macdonald's review surely ruffled Hoover's feathers: "It has been clear to me for a long time that J. Edgar Hoover is as adept at public relations as he and his G-men are inept at actual detective work." (The FBI memo quoted this passage from Macdonald's essay.)[32]

So Macdonald was investigated—yet again. The Bureau retraced the same old ground, but this time Macdonald stayed on the FBI's radar, if only intermittently. This monitoring coincided with Macdonald's renewed interest in U.S. politics, especially electoral politics. Macdonald was undergoing yet another sea change in his personal and professional life as the 1960s opened. He found his political interests revived in the new decade by the Vietnam anti-war movement and the student power movement. Now in his sixties, Macdonald was radicalized by these twin causes, both of which Hoover was convinced were controlled by the Communists.

For Macdonald, the 1960s became a heady replay of the 1930s. He admired the actions of the student protesters who took possession of university buildings, boycotted classes (and denounced unsympathetic faculty), and marched in pro–North Vietnamese demonstrations. Suffering from a severe writer's block and drinking heavily, he bristled on hearing expressions of worry from family and friends. Angrily declaring himself "an alcoholic, damn it," he embraced the movement, finding a radical cause again, responding to an inner voice calling him to mount a new barricade in the name of Revolution.[33] Macdonald also came to the attention of the FBI briefly in another context in the mid-1960s. The Bureau was asked to investigate him in 1965 when President Lyndon Johnson decided to hold a White House Festival of the Arts in June. Oddly, Macdonald had been placed on the guest list. Inviting Macdonald turned out to be a major mistake on Johnson's part: Macdonald cleverly exploited the event as a high-profile opportunity to militate against the war by gathering signatures for an anti–Vietnam War statement. Of course, from the point of view of the White House and those sympathetic to America's conduct of the war, Macdonald spent his visit making a general nuisance of himself.[34]

That is how the Johnson White House later downplayed it. Yet Johnson's ill-timed White House Festival of the Arts—a literary gala intended to emulate the Kennedy administration's courtship of the world of culture—represents a watershed moment in American intellectual history, and Macdonald put

Dwight Macdonald at La Salle College (now La Salle University), in Philadelphia.
Along with Frank S. Meyer, a prominent libertarian conservative and editor of
National Review, Macdonald participated in a panel discussion on "The Future
of American Politics" on November 15, 1963, just a week before John F. Kennedy's
assassination. Macdonald occasionally visited Philadelphia at the invitation of
his friend, the European historian John Lukacs, who taught part-time at the
college. As the 1960s wore on, Macdonald typically addressed political issues,
most often his opposition to the Johnson administration's escalation of American
involvement in the Vietnam War.

Courtesy: La Salle University Archives

in a show-stealing cameo appearance in the drama. For one brief and shining moment, as it were, the festival vouchsafed the exuberantly outspoken, irresistibly feisty Dwight Macdonald another fifteen minutes of fame and caused the vigilant gaze of the G-men to fall upon him. This last consequential episode in these odd-couple meetings between the earnest G-men and the *PR* highbrows further illuminates why the Bureau failed throughout the middle decades of the twentieth century, even as the Cold War thawed out, to understand the American left-wing intelligentsia in general and ex-Trotskyists such as the *PR* writers in particular.

As in the case of the Whittaker Chambers material in Lionel Trilling's FBI file, the documents related to this single event in which Macdonald enters in a walk-on role—the June 1965 festival—represent the highlight of Macdonald's dossier. Moreover, this section of Macdonald's FBI file spans almost one-fifth of the total (118 pages) and provides a fascinating glimpse into how the worlds of culture and politics intersected during the opening years of America's Vietnam saga. And this first and only White House Festival of the Arts stands today as the sole major example in modern America of a joint cooperative venture in the arts between the federal government and the intellectual elite. Indeed, the Kultur clash between the Johnson politicos and the liberal intellectuals in 1965 possesses broad implications today. It signaled the end of a period of mutual admiration between Democratic leaders in Washington and the liberal intelligentsia. Decades of suspicion and mistrust of liberal and radical intellectuals would follow, not only minimizing the impact of public intellectuals specifically but also bearing more widely on issues dealing with both government policies in the arts and standards of decorum in contemporary intellectual life.

A BAD FAIRY'S "DAY AT THE WHITE HOUSE"

A series of unforeseen developments propelled Macdonald to the epicenter of controversy in the spring of 1965 as the minidrama of the White House Festival of the Arts unfolded. A rejected invitation turned out to be the opening act—followed by a tragicomic climax and denouement.

Among those invited to the festival in late May 1965 was Robert Lowell, the much-admired New England Brahmin man of letters who was widely regarded as the unofficial poet laureate of the nation. Johnson's advisers selected Lowell to represent America's writers, and he initially accepted the White House invitation. But he had second thoughts after discussing the matter with some of his confreres in the literary-intellectual community, especially novelist Philip Roth and Robert Silvers, the coeditor of the *New*

WA079 PD
    KM NEWYORK NY 3 1225P EDT.
THE PRESIDENT
  THE WHITE HOUSE
DEAR PRESIDENT JOHNSON: WE WHO HAVE CONSIDERED OURSELVES
FRIENDS OF THE ADMINISTRATION SUPPORT ROBERT LOWELL IN HIS
DECISION NOT TO PARTICIPATE IN THE WHITE HOUSE FESTIVAL OF
THE ARTS ON JUNE 14TH. THOUGH HE HAS SPOKEN ONLY FOR HIMSELF,
WE WOULD LIKE YOU TO KNOW THAT OTHERS OF US SHARE HIS DISMAY
AT RECENT AMERICAN FOREIGN POLICY DECISIONS. WE HOPE THAT

PEOPLE IN THIS AND IN OTHER COUNTRIES WILL NOT CONCLUDE
THAT A WHITE HOUSE ARTS PROGRAM TESTIFIES TO APPROVAL OF
ADMINISTRATION POLICY BY THE MEMBERS OF THE ARTISTIC COMMUNITY.
TO THE CONTRARY, AS THE WEEKS PASS SOME OF US HAVE BECOME MORE AND
MORE ALARMED BY A STANCE IN FOREIGN AFFAIRS WHICH SEEMS INCREASINGLY
BELLIGERENT AND MILITARISTIC,
HANNAH ARENDT

ALFRED KAZIN

Twenty artists and intellectuals, including Alfred Kazin, signed a telegram sent to the Johnson White House in support of Robert Lowell's June 1965 decision not to participate in the Festival of the Arts. Their reason, which Lowell had also voiced, was that they had become "more and more alarmed by a stance in foreign affairs which seems increasingly belligerent and militaristic." They were, of course, referring to the escalation of American participation in the Vietnam War. All the names are blacked out in the FBI file except for Hannah Arendt, whose name appears first because the signers had listed themselves in alphabetical order. (Kazin's name is not blacked out in his own file.)

York Review of Books. In early June, Lowell sent a rejection to Eric Goldman, the Johnson White House's "intellectual in residence" and the planner of the gala. Lowell also published a letter in the June 3 *New York Times* that expressed his disapproval of the administration's foreign and military policies, especially the escalation of the Vietnam War, which was turning America into "an explosive and suddenly chauvinistic nation." Addressing the president personally, Lowell continued, "Although I am very enthusiastic about most of your domestic legislation and intentions, I nevertheless can only follow our present foreign policy with the greatest dismay and distrust. . . . I know it is hard for the responsible man to act; it is also painful for the private and irresolute man to dare criticism. At this anguished, delicate and perhaps determining moment, I feel I am serving you and our country best by not taking part in the White House Festival of the Arts."

At this point Macdonald was invited to the festival as a representative of the intellectual community. The letter of invitation had obviously gone out before Lowell's statement appeared in the *New York Times*, which his supporters backed by sending a telegram to Johnson. On June 4, the *Times* printed the telegram, endorsed by Macdonald and twenty other distinguished signatories, including Hannah Arendt, John Berryman, Lillian Hellman, Bernard Malamud, Alfred Kazin, Philip Roth, Mary McCarthy, Mark Rothko, and Robert Penn Warren. Having cosigned as an expression of support for Lowell, Macdonald was now in a quandary. He had not expected to receive a White House invitation and was not sure what to do. Yes, he realized, consistency would have required him to reject the invitation. But to repeat: consistency had never been Dwight's strong suit.

No, controversy was. Macdonald therefore decided to attend the festival, as he later insisted in "A Day at the White House" (his seven-thousand-word piece that ran in the *New York Review of Books* on July 15, 1965), so that at least one critical observer "would be there to report on just what went on." It was, he conceded, "a complicated, inconsistent, perhaps absurd tactic," but he deemed it essential to have added at least one "bad fairy at the christening." Or as he later wrote, "I sacrificed, not for the first time, consistency, and possibly even good taste, in the interest of a larger objective."[35]

Eric Goldman at the White House was perplexed. His fresh and wondrous idea was rapidly turning sour. He believed that Macdonald "hoped I would disinvite him" because he supported Lowell's protest. When Macdonald asked if he was still welcome, Goldman replied that "he had been invited without any test of his attitude toward the president's foreign policy—in fact, with full knowledge of his hostility to the Vietnam War."[36] Such a statement was very noble but also more than a bit naive. For as practically all of cultural

New York had known for decades, Macdonald was invariably a loose cannon prone to firing off in all directions. Or more: Dwight could be dynamite.

With respect to at least one significant detail, however, Goldman was not fully candid with Macdonald. Goldman did not explain that before issuing the invitation, the White House—acting at the behest of a key Johnson adviser, Marvin Watson, the president's top hatchet man—had ordered an FBI check of Macdonald and the other potential invitees.

The FBI dossier covering mid-1965 on Macdonald (repeatedly misspelled here as *McDonald*) furnishes keen insight into the mentality of a Johnson White House already under siege as the Vietnam conflict heated up. The file also reveals how the FBI investigated and monitored the intellectuals. The file is comprehensive: in addition to editors at the *New Yorker*, *Commentary*, Random House, and other publications, the two senators from New York, Jacob K. Javits and Robert F. Kennedy, were interviewed about Macdonald. Twenty-three other persons, including professional associates, social acquaintances, and former and present neighbors were also interviewed.

Yet Macdonald's file is at the same time rather amateurish and off-target. The reason for the ineptitude is that the FBI was plunging into largely uncharted waters, probing a cultural world about which its agents were almost totally ignorant. The FBI dutifully gathered information on Macdonald from his birth to the present. But the outcome was a compendium of the comical and the trifling. For example, one FBI memo noted that in January 1958, Macdonald addressed a forum of the "Young Socialists League" in New York on the topic of "mass culture versus high culture." A January 28, 1965, memo reiterates the old misinformation that Macdonald "was well-known in communist circles, under the name of McCarthy." But the memo elaborates on the 1944 file, making clear that "communist" encompassed Trotskyism for the reporting G-man: "The Albany office of the FBI also interviewed a former communist revolutionary in Birmingham, AL who had known Macdonald. His name was Hall, and Macdonald had visited Birmingham to research a *Fortune* article. Hall briefed Macdonald on the labor picture locally as background for the article." Macdonald was "not friendly to Hall at the time," which "might have been due to [blacked out] Party connections. Macdonald had a reputation as a Trotzkyite [*sic*] at the time." (The FBI agent repeatedly writes "Trotzkyite.")

That spelling howler would have amused Macdonald to no end—and perhaps even elicited a boffo essay on political language either to match his sterling critiques of the Revised Standard Bible and of Vice President Henry Wallace's speechmaking or to rival Macdonald's brilliant parodies of Hemingway's later prose style and of Douglas MacArthur's foul-mouthed pep talks to the troops. The rationale for ordering an extensive FBI background check on Macdonald was equally risible. It was occasioned not by his invitation to the upcoming gala. Rather—amazingly enough—the White House was considering Macdonald for a position in the administration's anti-poverty program. "And if this be the case," one informant told FBI agents, Macdonald "would be a highly suitable choice for such a program."

If one takes that recommendation straight—rather than as an attempt to feed the G-men a line—its basis can only be Macdonald's *New Yorker* cover story on poverty in early 1962 and his well-known radical sympathies for the underclass. And it is certainly true that Macdonald played a cameo part in the launching of the anti-poverty program by popularizing Michael Harrington's book on the state of the poor, *The Other America* (1962). One of Macdonald's associates at *Esquire*, probably publisher Arnold Gingrich (all names are blacked out in the FBI files but the context suggests Gingrich), informed the Bureau that Macdonald's review of *The Other America* had come to President Kennedy's personal attention and sparked Johnson's War on Poverty.[37]

Perhaps Macdonald's intellectual friends at the White House from their times together in New York—among them trusted Kennedy advisers who were still in positions at the Johnson White House, such as Arthur Schlesinger Jr. and John Kenneth Galbraith—had drawn JFK's attention to Macdonald's *New Yorker* essay.[38] Nonetheless, the notion that Macdonald might have been seriously under consideration for a staff position in the Johnson administration, serving in a program that would become the cornerstone of the president's Great Society, stretches credulity. In fact, the thought that Macdonald, by nature a crotchety malcontent and maverick, would be considered for any bureaucratic appointment, is quite beyond imagination.

This portion of Macdonald's FBI file makes especially fun reading. Several memos expressed indignation that Macdonald was critical of "the FBI and the director," noting that he had edited *politics* and that the magazine's winter 1948 issue "contained a vicious attack on the director and the Bureau from a self-styled anarchist [Clifton Bennett] who received a five-year sentence in 1945 as a draft dodger." The FBI memo also mentioned that Macdonald had "falsely criticized the FBI" in his November 1962 *Esquire* review of *Experiment in Terror*.

But the FBI agents did not simply zero in on Macdonald's criticisms of Hoover and his men. They sniffed throughout the country for information about Macdonald's past. They did a decent job of assembling a thumbnail biography of Macdonald and a detailed chronology of his manifold activities. Still, their unfamiliarity with both the complex history of American radicalism and of the arcane subtleties of left-wing sectarian politics steered them onto some strange and misdirected byways.

The G-men correctly established the basic facts of Macdonald's life, family background, and education. When they discussed the implications and significance of this material, however, they often went astray. For example, they correctly noted that Macdonald worked for *Fortune* in the early 1930s but listed him as one of its founders, a point that would surely have surprised both his employer, Henry Luce, the real founder, and Macdonald himself.

In another report, the FBI accurately wrote that Macdonald had a long record of opposing Soviet communism and was highly critical of Stalin. But here in particular, they were obviously uninformed about the nuances of American radical politics. Some of the sources whom they interviewed for information about Macdonald gave implausible interpretations of his various shifts in political positions, which Bureau agents reported as if they were indisputable facts.

For example, one source, probably Philip Rahv, editor of *Partisan Review*—here again, the name is blacked out yet the context indicates Rahv—pulled the FBI's leg with several bits of amusing disinformation. He told the FBI not only that Macdonald was "anti-communist, anti-Stalinist, and anti–Red Chinese" (accurate) but also that *politics*—Macdonald's radical magazine advocating "anarcho-pacifism"—was "strictly of the non-political type." Given the journal's title, this statement is quite a whopper. Moreover, since the charge "nonpolitical" was precisely the accusation that Macdonald had fired off in *politics* against *Partisan Review*'s increasing emphasis on cultural and artistic topics in the early post-war era, the report shows Rahv's own love of vengeful mischief and much-underrated sense of roguish humor—both well-known Macdonald trademarks. The same source also described Macdonald as an "amateur anarchist." The FBI agents recorded this observation but made no comment on it. Either they took it also at face value or, perhaps more plausibly, had no clear idea what the term meant.

Continuing the playful disinformation, a number of informants described Macdonald as an upstanding citizen and even "a loyal American." A *New Yorker* colleague stated that "nothing had ever come to his attention during the past thirteen years which would cause him to question the appointee's morals, political affiliations, or choice of associates." This colleague knew of "no reason why the appointee should not be placed in a position of trust with the United States government." Another *New Yorker* colleague stated that "the appointee is one of the greatest literary critics in the United States today" and that "his intellectual curiosity and his ability to write his thoughts are unquestioned," though he "never looked upon [Macdonald] as a very conventional individual." Still another *New Yorker* colleague stated, "Macdonald and members of his family are individuals of excellent character and ones who are loyal American citizens." The source also laughably maintained that Macdonald "has always handled himself in an excellent manner and has always been well-behaved," further claiming "that Macdonald does not drink alcoholic beverages to any extent." Even Macdonald's casual acquaintances were well aware that such statements were ludicrous. Delivering more half-truths, the informant described Macdonald as having a rather flamboyant personality, as a person who likes to argue a point for the sake of argument. However, Macdonald was always pleasant during these periods of argumentation. Indeed, for anyone who knew Macdonald even slightly, perhaps just a single encounter at a social gathering, these statements in toto amount to an hilariously absurd portrait. They could in fact form the basis for a wondrously unforgettable humorous essay à la Macdonald's bravo sendups, which even extended to literary lightweights such as James Gould Cozzens and Colin Wilson.

An editor at *Commentary* (probably Norman Podhoretz, who worked closely with Macdonald on a few pieces) was also interviewed. This editor, too, emphasized that Macdonald was "anti-communist and anti-Stalin" and that "there is no question of Macdonald's loyalty to the United States." The FBI agent noted approvingly that *Commentary* is "one of America's foremost anti-communist periodicals."

A reference at Random House, probably Jason Epstein, another member of the New York Intellectual circle, told the Bureau that he had known Macdonald for twelve years and that he was "a man of high morals and character. His reputation in the literary field has been above reproach." The FBI memo concluded that this interviewee "would recommend him as a loyal citizen capable of assuming a position of trust and responsibility."

A source at New York University, possibly James Burnham (who had belonged to the same Trotskyist sect as Macdonald in the 1930s), reported that he had known Macdonald since the mid-1930s and that he "is the type of writer who writes what he believes, and if he has been wronged he would turn around and write that which was correct. Macdonald has always written on anything regardless of what it was, just so long as he believed in it." Another interviewee also spoke about Macdonald in similar terms, telling the FBI that he had known Macdonald professionally and socially for more than twenty years and that he is "a person of the highest integrity" and is "incapable of telling a lie."

Among other aspects of its data gathering, the FBI tracked down the numerous places where Macdonald had lived, his trips abroad, how he had voted in past elections, and where he had banked and what his credit status was.[39] (The Bureau even checked up on his brother, Hedges, a conservative banker who was a vice president of Northern Trust Company in Chicago.)

Always a fierce critic of corporate capitalism, probably the cavalier, improv-

The FBI interviewed at least twenty-five individuals for information about
Macdonald as part of a White House background check. Among the references
were both former classmates at Yale University and fellow intellectuals associated
with the leading magazines of the 1960s. All of the references recommended
Macdonald unhesitatingly; he was "a loyal citizen capable of assuming a position
of trust and responsibility." One of the sources apparently was Mary McCarthy,
who "recommended the appointee very highly for any position of trust and
confidence." Likely these sources were tweaking the nose of the FBI agents.
Surely some of his intellectual contemporaries were well aware of his notorious
1958 article in *Twentieth Century* in which Macdonald specifically repudiated
the intended praise of a British editor that he was a "Good American," insisting
instead that he was (in his own proud phrase) a "Critical American."

ident Macdonald would have laughed about the fact that he had an excellent credit rating. Macdonald's favorable record probably resulted from his years of marriage to his first wife, the wealthy radical activist Nancy Rodman, whose inheritance had bankrolled *politics* (and whom Dwight's magazine had virtually bankrupted by the time of its demise in 1949). The FBI also investigated the couple's divorce, documenting the court records and interviewing several participants in the proceedings.[40] They found nothing sensational or embarrassing about the divorce. In fact, after initially refusing to be interviewed, Nancy cooperated fully and said only positive things about her ex-husband.

As part of its investigation, the FBI also contacted the two senators from New York, Macdonald's home state. Javits, a liberal Republican, voiced a highly favorable opinion of Macdonald, though Kennedy claimed to have no knowledge of Macdonald. This was disingenuous, to say the least. As Michael Wreszin points out in his superb biography of Macdonald, *A Rebel in Defense of Tradition* (1994), Macdonald and Kennedy had exchanged correspondence early in 1965, with Macdonald prodding the senator to denounce Johnson's Vietnam policy.

However improbable, the FBI's final report on Macdonald was wholly approving. The overall judgment was that Macdonald was a distinguished literary critic with strong opinions who was beyond doubt a "loyal American." His vociferous attacks on the Bureau and on Hoover himself went mysteriously unmentioned.[41]

When the Festival of the Arts opened on June 14, 1965, therefore, White House officials believed that everything would go smoothly and that they had a good idea of what to expect from Macdonald and the other guests. In his memoir of his White House years, *The Tragedy of Lyndon Johnson*, however, Goldman claims that he wasn't so confident. True, he was buoyed by the fact that he had gathered a distinguished cross section of the American intellectual community. The list included first-rate novelists (John Hersey and Saul Bellow), respected poets (Mark Van Doren and Phyllis McGinley), a few recognized painters and sculptors (Mark Rothko), plus the main speaker for the festival (the renowned conscience of American foreign policy, George Kennan). Despite this impressive lineup, however, Goldman had been worried about the festival for months—since the February letter in the *New York Times* from Lowell and the other signatories. Johnson himself took a dim view of the proceedings, distancing himself from the planning details, adopting a pose of Olympian disdain, and all the while expecting the worst from those East Coast liberals whom he typically referred to as "the Harvards." (The event was officially hosted and organized by Lady Bird Johnson.)[42]

The White House social secretary, old Johnson friend Bess Abell, immediately put her finger on the problem on hearing about Goldman's idea. "These people," she remarked of the intellectuals, "can be troublesome."[43]

How right she would prove to be! And none of "these people" more fully amounted to a life-size, walking, gesticulating, radicalized definition of "troublesome"—complete with anachronistic Leninist goatee—than Dwight Macdonald.

A MACDONALD "SPECTACULAR": "EYEBALL TO EYEBALL" WITH CHARLTON HESTON

On June 14, Macdonald arrived in Washington armed with a statement he had drafted (along with Tom Hess of *Art News*) announcing that attendance at the festival in no way signified support for the administration's foreign policy. Throughout the day and into the evening, an increasingly disheveled Macdonald—he was wearing a rumpled suit, white shirt sans tie, and tennis shoes for the occasion—buttonholed (and in at least one exchange challenged and provoked) other invitees, asking them to sign his petition.

Macdonald never shied away from making a scene—indeed, making scenes was a Macdonald specialty—and his behavior during his infamous "Day at the White House" led, not surprisingly, to unpleasant run-ins with several of the guests. African American novelist Ralph Ellison spurned Macdonald, calling his actions "arrogant." The painter Peter Hurd objected that circulating a critical petition "when you are a house guest is just plain uncivilized." Saul Bellow, after first agreeing to sign, reconsidered on the same grounds, arguing that it was an offensive way to act as a guest in someone's house. (Macdonald countered that the White House belonged not to Johnson but to all Americans.)[44] In a 1975 letter, Macdonald criticized Bellow's "flimsy/odd reasons" for attending and reading at the White House Festival: "To confront the truth/actuality of his role at the Festival would have forced Saul to the kind of new self-understanding and rejection of his old values that Ivan Ilyich had to make."[45] Years later, in an interview with Michael Wreszin, Bellow—a *Partisan Review* contributor and close colleague of several New York Intellectuals who was already shifting rightward in reaction to the counterculture and escalating anti–Vietnam War protests—lashed back. He countered that Macdonald "pranced into the rose-garden like Pan in tennis shoes—a sex-symbol on a political mission."[46] (Macdonald was also the object of Bellow's satire in *Humboldt's Gift*, appearing in the figure of Orlando Higgins, the nudist proselyte and intellectual lightweight.)

Macdonald had his most direct and disagreeable encounter with the actor Charlton Heston, who arrived just after performing another one of his many screen roles featuring world historical figures (in this case Michelangelo). Heston was a featured guest at the festival: the administration had selected him to close the daytime program by serving as narrator for a short documentary celebrating post–World War II American cinema. Heston and Macdonald got into a shouting match about the appropriateness of Macdonald's behavior. (Macdonald was always good at raising the decibel level in his discussions.) When Heston refused to sign the petition, according to an organizer of the event who witnessed the exchange, Macdonald pilloried Heston as "a lowbrow lackey of Hollywood."[47] According to Macdonald, Heston said during their "eyeball-to-eyeball confrontation in the Rose Garden" that Macdonald's actions showed an utter lack of manners and that it was "arrogant" for "mere" intellectuals (*mere* was Macdonald's word) to question the administration's foreign policy. After all, claimed Heston, the White House and the State Department "must" know more about international affairs and about what the country needed than did Dwight Macdonald and his radical cronies.[48]

Although Macdonald professed not to harbor any disappointment, his petition had little success. He and Hess approached between forty and fifty people, and only a handful signed: Goldman says seven, Macdonald nine.[49] Goldman claims a certain vindication for his brainchild by noting that more than four hundred people attended the festival, yet only a handful endorsed Macdonald's petition. Or as Lady Bird Johnson later cracked, "I'll take a 397 to 7 majority any time."[50] Yet in the higher calculus of American cultural politics, that landslide margin equated to nothing more than a pyrrhic victory. The numbers really added up to a public relations "disaster" (Goldman's word) among the intelligentsia and glitterati.[51]

Macdonald seemed quite pleased with his performance, however. By supporting Lowell's protest, he believed that he and Hess had sent a jarring message that spread dismay within the White House. Macdonald ended his essay on the festival by quoting Alexander Herzen's observation about a literary attack against the reactionary Tsar Nicholas I: "It was a shot that rang out in the dark night. . . . It forced us all to awaken."[52]

If so, the slumbering Johnson White House awoke to a hellish nightmare—and the aftereffects of Macdonald's actions proved more complicated than he allowed in his retrospective on the day. The Johnson administration's decision to sponsor the festival tumbled the president and his advisers into a policymaking disaster in the world of culture that would soon escalate into a proto-Vietnam—this time, of course, a quagmire on the home front pitting him anew against another hated enemy to the north, Johnson's domestic bête noire, the liberal East Coast intelligentsia.

The hubbub before and during the festival doomed such events for the future. Presidents Ronald Reagan and Bill Clinton invited entertainers and musicians galore—ranging from Frank Sinatra to Willie Nelson—but no administration in the past five decades has possessed the assurance (or the audacity) to invite a disparate troupe of politically minded intellectuals and artists to the White House. The risks of another smashup have seemed too great.

That fact, too, is part of the "tragedy"—the word is strong yet not exaggerated. Goldman's high-minded dream of bringing together the worlds of politics and culture crashed around him. It appears in hindsight as the pivotal event marking the break between the government and the nation's leading critical intellectuals. From another angle, the failure of the White House Festival represents the first historical signpost on the road to ruin between the American presidency and the intellectuals as it races downward from the Vietnam War era to the Watergate Affair between 1965 and 1974. Although the Reagan White House of the 1980s and later Republican administrations have been quite hospitable to right-wing intellectuals—especially the neoconservatives—liberal intellectuals have experienced an enduring alienation from Washington, with only liberal policy wonks developing close relationships with later Democratic administrations.[53]

Despite his breezy piece about the festival in the *New York Review of Books*, Macdonald himself had second thoughts about his White House conduct, composing two letters that indicate that he privately reevaluated his behavior and judged it less than tasteful. Writing to his son, Nick, on July 6, 1965, Macdonald defended his actions during the White House visit. Nick essentially echoed the criticism of his father's opponents, arguing that it was not right to come "as a guest to some place, only to run around and knife him in the back." Dwight replied that the festival was a public event and "those who attended it had a right to express . . . their disenchantment with the things being done in Vietnam and Santo Domingo." Dwight did admit that he might have been wrong to circulate the petition against Johnson. But he maintained, "I decided it was at least as much a public celebration as a private affair."[54]

Macdonald also backtracked somewhat in a December 8, 1965, private letter to his closest friend, Nicola Chiaromonte, who chided him for his behavior at the festival. Macdonald admitted that Chiaromonte's criticisms hit home. But then Macdonald made light of the entire incident and dismissed *Time*'s report on the festival, which had also chastised him for acting in poor taste.

In a letter of protest to *Time*, Macdonald said its account omitted his waggish remark about his grounds for attending: "I like to review spectaculars and this one promised to be even more spectacular than *Ben Hur* and *King of Kings* put together"—a good line that gains additional resonance in view of Macdonald's shouting match with Charlton Heston, the star of *Ben Hur*.[55]

MEMORIAL FOR A REVOLUTIONIST

The 1965 White House Festival of the Arts represents the closing act of Macdonald's colorful and controversy-laden career and the final instance of the FBI's close attention to him. As the 1960s progressed, Macdonald increasingly displaced his prodigious critical energies into anti-war activism: his return to the radicalism of his youth was largely an attempt to distract himself from his literary impotence and dependence on the bottle. By the mid-1960s and even more so in the 1970s, he found it nearly impossible to complete any intellectual projects he had undertaken—and his journals show that he lacerated himself mercilessly for this failure. He wrote very little of any consequence during his last dozen years. In 1967 he gave up reviewing movies for *Esquire* to write a monthly political column; it soon petered out. Instead, he began teaching at various colleges and universities, which gave him a perfect excuse for reneging on his prior literary commitments and declining new assignments.

Why were anti-war activism and college teaching not enough to fulfill Macdonald? By all accounts, he was an excellent teacher. Beginning in 1956, he taught both at major universities and at commuter campuses, among them Northwestern University, Bard College, the University of Massachusetts at Amherst, the University of California at Santa Cruz, the University of Wisconsin at Milwaukee, Hofstra University, the State University of New York at Buffalo (for several semesters), and John Jay College of the City University of New York. When he taught in 1966 at the University of Texas at Austin as a distinguished visiting professor (with feigned patrician pretentiousness, he delighted to cite his academic title), he was sometimes the only faculty member at campus rallies sponsored by the local SDS chapter. Excited to listen to *Esquire*'s movie critic discourse on contemporary cinema, the students enjoyed his course on film history. Both the *Daily Texan* and the *Austin American-Statesman* were filled with reports of his political pronouncements, and several *Daily Texan* pieces featured him on the front page.[56]

But this was not enough. Macdonald's fundamental identity was that of a writer. He regarded teaching as a sideline—he was "like a tennis bum" at universities, he felt, because teaching was "more output than input"—rather "like mining, an extractive industry," not a productive activity such as farming or manufacturing.[57] As he wrote in one journal entry in the 1970s, "I am a writer and I must keep in contact with my mother earth, or like Antaeus I begin to die. If character is destiny, MY character is a monochrome = 100% writing."[58] During one of his frequent attempts to find a visiting professorship, he wrote to a friend that he wanted desperately to teach because his flow of written words was "dammed to a trickle."[59] And Macdonald damned himself for that. He demanded from himself "100% writing." And so—like Antaeus—he began to die.

Nobody was tougher on Macdonald's unproductivity than Macdonald himself. By contrast, his editors and publishers were far more understanding, even though by the mid-1970s, Macdonald seldom delivered on a writing commitment—not the study of mass culture, not the book on Edgar Allan Poe, and above all not his long-planned intellectual autobiography. He could do little more than relive the past by updating or gathering together old work—for example, adding a few postscripts to a reprint of a selection of his old *politics* pieces (originally published as *Memoirs of a Revolutionist*, 1957) and collecting in a separate volume some of his later essays (*Discriminations*, 1974). It was all due to his "Bartleby neurosis," he told one scholar in 1973 as he backed out of a promise to write a preface to her critical study of Poe, explaining (in his biographer's words) that he "could not write anything more than a letter—and not many of them either."[60]

The coup de grâce had been quietly delivered a few months earlier. In 1972, a supremely patient William Shawn, editor of the *New Yorker*, finally insisted that the lovable "Dwight" relinquish his office; Macdonald had written nothing in the magazine for nearly a decade. His participation in the protest movement of the 1960s was his way of investing his life with a new, enlarged significance. But he was just a marginal figure in the protest scene as far as the FBI was concerned. Additions to his file dwindled as the decade advanced.

The FBI followed Macdonald's anti-war agitation of the 1960s but mentioned him only in passing. For example, when fifty people walked out in protest against a 1967 speech by Vice President Hubert Humphrey before the National Book Conference, the Bureau noted that Macdonald was among the protesters. In December 1969, Macdonald and Dr. Benjamin Spock participated in an anti-war march on the Department of Justice. Once there, he beseeched young men to turn in their draft cards as a form of protest. FBI agents investigated him once again—this time for organizing draft dodgers—but decided that since Macdonald "is not a member of any basic revolutionary group, no recommendation is being made at this time for inclusion of his name in the Security Index."[61]

Ironically, it was a repeat of the story from a decade earlier: "Who is he?" Macdonald couldn't ever get the FBI to take him seriously for very long. And so, much to his likely disappointment—if he had known—Macdonald quietly faded from the FBI's attention after 1970, much as he also did from the national intellectual and literary scenes. Sporadically memorialized by the publications for which he had once served as a mainstay, he died in December 1982 of congestive heart failure, largely a forgotten man.[62] His fame had passed long ago. He was an old-fashioned libertarian deemed no longer relevant—either to his "herd" of fellow intellectuals or even to the FBI agents who snooped on them all.

FROM LUCE TO LENIN TO LENNON

Macdonald's celebration of the counterculture of the 1960s, which extended even to enthusiasm for the Yippies and for the student demonstrators who occupied professors' offices and closed down colleges, confused the FBI even as it disturbed (or outraged) many of his New York Intellectual colleagues (particularly Irving Kristol and Sidney Hook, both of whom were shifting sharply rightward by this time).

In hindsight, Macdonald erred in his blithe enthusiasm for the student radicals and counterculture faddists, whereby he undermined the very traditions and norms of excellence that he otherwise championed. Such misjudgments represented a political and moral surrender that has had long-term, disastrous consequences. The counterculture of the 1960s has given rise to the anti-intellectualism that currently pervades the American academy, which has witnessed the ascendancy of intellectually fashionable theories such as multiculturalism, postmodernism, and poststructuralism. Furthermore, that decade marked the beginning of the eclipse of serious print culture by the pop cultures of video and MTV. Today infotainment, soft porn, and debased language infest our cultural life. One encounters them everywhere, vomited by an indolent, sensation-seeking media whose barrages of images and sounds displace the written word. The outcome of all this slovenliness is a zombie-like state of shallow thinking bereft of introspection, "the gramophone mind," in the phrase of George Orwell, Macdonald's cherished pen friend and *politics* contributor.[63]

Macdonald's career is both an exemplar and an omen for us today. As was true for Lionel Trilling, it is no surprise that the FBI, whose agents were seldom versed in the dialectical disputes within the sectarian Left—let alone in the nuances of intellectual debates in New York—did not comprehend such a nonpareil individualist as Macdonald. They failed to appreciate how he was,

The photo originally appeared in *Columbia Today* under the title "Anarchist Dwight Macdonald." The larger, official Columbia University commencement was relocated for security reasons to the Cathedral of St. John the Divine. The so-called countercommencement occurred on June 4, 1968.

Courtesy: Columbia College Today

if not a "Good American," indeed a "Critical American." Macdonald's complicated sociopolitical coordinates, short-lived impassioned enthusiasms, and seemingly inexplicable lurches of allegiance every few years—from Luce to Lenin to Lennon, as it were—did not make it any easier for Hoover's G-men. His seismic ideological shifts—from mainstream liberalism to radical libertarianism to "anarcho-pacifism" to "I Choose the West" pro-Americanism to (finally) SDS/counterculture activism—baffled the FBI even as it frustrated the majority of Macdonald's rightward-turning coevals. Most of them patronized "Dwight" as a political thinker because he seemed to wax hot and turn cold with alarming and unpredictable frequency. Virtually all his colleagues were much steadier and more sober in their political commitments.

Both his admirers and his detractors today should understand all this about the dazzling, dappled, sometimes darkish rainbow of selves that populated Macdonald's conflicted inner life. The whole man possessed and often gloried in his apparent contradictions, for he "contained multitudes," in Whitman's phrase, that included both the bracing cultural critiques and the sometimes ill-considered ideological enthusiasms. The latter ought not to obscure the former. However we assess the FBI's surveillance of him, that fact is vital in coming to terms with Macdonald himself.

Nor should Macdonald's sad end invalidate his three decades of outspoken, often solitary protest as an eloquent dissident voice writing "against the American grain" (in his 1962 essay collection of that title).[64] His years as a one-man magazine staff in the mid- to late 1940s, when he edited *politics*, shine forth as a radiant example of how an intellectual both becomes a national resource and may serve as moral conscience and voice in the wilderness. Present-day readers and writers need to keep alive the unbowed critical spirit and lonely intellectual courage, notwithstanding his sometimes unfortunate political judgment and misplaced social idealism, that Dwight Macdonald exemplified at his best.

And his best—in his politics and his *politics*, as he both lived it and wrote it—was very good indeed. It remains a summons and inspiration for concerned citizens today.

Irving Howe in his office at Stanford University, 1962.
Courtesy: Nina Howe

CHAPTER FOUR

WANTED BY THE FBI?

IRVING HORENSTEIN, #7384A AKA "REVOLUTIONARY CONSPIRATOR" IRVING HOWE

TAILING A "TROTSKYITE"

The file on Irving Howe (né Horenstein) compiled by the Federal Bureau of Investigation (FBI) discloses that its agents followed his activities closely for more than eight years. It searched his records extensively, interviewed neighbors and colleagues to uncover information about his activities, and pursued him as a national security risk long after he had resigned from the Independent Socialist League (ISL), a tiny, New York–based Trotskyist sect.[1] The file contains 148 pages, 15 of them partially or wholly blacked out. It runs from February 27, 1951, to April 14, 1959, and covers reports from regional FBI bureaus in New York City, Albany, Newark, St. Louis, Miami, Boston, and Detroit.[2]

Most of these reports address Howe's activities in the ISL and his membership in Trotskyist organizations in the 1940s and 1950s. Much of the file covers Howe's statements in public lectures about the Soviet Union and regarding the changing nature of Stalinism during the 1950s. One glaring feature of the file is conspicuous by its absence, though it is perhaps by now unsurprising. As with Lionel Trilling and Dwight Macdonald, the fact that no agent ever seems to have read any of Howe's work to ascertain his political positions speaks volumes about the one-size-fits-all information-gathering procedures of the American intelligence services during the Cold War. The sole exception is the joint resignation letter that he and Stanley Plastrik submitted to the ISL in 1952, a copy of which was obtained by a Bureau informant.

For historians and scholars, one irony in Howe's dossier that he would doubtless have appreciated is that FBI agents (however unaware of the irony) repeatedly call him, using the same invidious language as did his Cold War-era Stalinist opponents, a *Trotskyite*, a term that also occasionally surfaces (along with *Trotzkyite*) in Macdonald's dossier. The Feds used the labels *Trotskyist* and *Trotskyite* interchangeably. Communist Party sympathizers knew better. They wielded the latter characterization as a cudgel. But the G-men failed to recognize any distinction between the two words.

The highlight of the FBI file on Howe (a name that the Bureau persisted in treating as his "alias" although Howe had legally changed it in 1948) is the hour-long interview that two agents sprung on him in August 1954.[3] When they approached him as he entered his car on a street in Cambridge, Massachusetts, the agents were impressed by his "friendly and cordial manner," though they later urged that a Security Index file be opened on him for long-term surveillance. Although Howe was never again confronted directly, the FBI kept watch on him for five more years. Reports continued to be placed in his file on his lectures to university audiences and to political clubs and even on his "luggage lost in France" during a trip to Europe in 1957.[4]

Howe's FBI file also furnishes a valuable biographical background for his repeated castigation of McCarthyism in the 1950s: it shows that Howe himself was being "tailed." After his semipublic "street interview" with the two FBI agents, if not long before, he certainly suspected as much. Such information puts in context his radical critique of U.S. policies and at the same time undermines part of the ad hominem neoconservative attack on his writings during the McCarthy period. Many of Howe's critics have argued that his 1954 essay, "This Age of Conformity," reflected his hypersensitivity regarding First Amendment freedoms. These critics imply that Howe harbored excessive and even irrational fears about government infringement on American civil liberties and about encroachments on personal privacy. His first biographer, Edward Alexander, refers to Howe's "compulsive . . . indictment of liberals who fail to take seriously the threat to civil liberties."[5]

Yet Howe's FBI file makes clear that in his case, this supposed compulsiveness actually constituted appropriate vigilance.[6] The criticism that he and *PR* writers such as Alfred Kazin expressed about the House Un-American Activities Committee (HUAC) and the Smith Act (formally known as the Alien Registration Act) in the 1950s still holds up six decades later.[7] The organizations classified as "revolutionary" under the Smith Act included a pair of Trotskyist groups to which Howe belonged, the SWP and ISL.

In fact, as I mentioned in chapter 1, Howe's lectures were secretly visited by Bureau agents or informants, his mail was intercepted and opened, and his

Alfred Kazin at Cape Cod with son, Michael, and (second) wife, Ann Birstein, in the mid-1950s, around the time when he began to support campaigns on the left to abolish the House Un-American Activities Committee.

Courtesy: Michael Kazin

daily activities were regularly reported and updated (residential addresses, phone number, magazine subscriptions). This eavesdropping continued for almost seven years after his formal resignation from the ISL. In addition, Howe's second wife, Thalia Phillies Howe, was subject to investigation during her years as a teacher at Miss Fine's Day School in Princeton.

Although he was apparently unaware during the 1950s and 1960s that the FBI was engaged in such wide-ranging surveillance of his and his family's private life, Howe would likely not have been surprised. According to the FBI reports of that afternoon in August 1954 when the two special agents suddenly stopped him on the street, he was quite "affable," "friendly," and "cordial" throughout the session.

Still, Howe's intellectual integrity forbade him from equating these invasions of his privacy (and indeed infringements on his and his family's civil liberties) with conditions in the USSR or in Soviet-occupied Eastern Europe either before or after Stalin's death in March 1953. Howe and *Dissent*, which he cofounded with Stanley Plastrik in January 1954—and whose launch may have prompted the FBI interview a few months later—not only fearlessly and relentlessly castigated McCarthy and his supporters but also inveighed against the U.S. government's abuse of the Smith Act, as Howe also did so directly to the two FBI agents who interviewed him.

Both Howe and *Dissent* subscribed to a "moderate" radicalism. At no time was Irving Howe a breast-beating, shrill critic of American domestic life, let alone an incendiary, flame-throwing radical extremist—in fact, his frustration with such compulsions on the Left, especially as voiced against the New Left from the mid-1960s on, led to his vilification by the leaders of Students for a Democratic Society (SDS) and by influential counterculture figures. His derision for the New Left never ingratiated him with the political mainstream or with conservatives.[8]

While Howe and *Dissent* deplored the domestic conduct of the FBI and some other government agencies, it was far from his intention to compare their cavalier treatment of American civil liberties with the arbitrary lawlessness of Communist police states. Like Dwight Macdonald, for whom Howe had worked as an assistant at *politics* in the 1940s (even serving briefly on the editorial board), the Irving Howe of the *Dissent* years was "a Critical American" in the sense of opposing any political position that rubber-stamped American domestic security policies or insisted that civic duty entailed uncritical celebration of the "American Way of Life." Howe never felt that his career was imperiled as a result of his public derision of McCarthyism, and he insisted on distinguishing the relatively mild abuses of U.S. government intelligence agencies from the despotic practices of the Soviet security forces. Nor did Howe ever equate the injustices suffered by some American radicals with how Soviet and East European intellectuals might be subject willy-nilly to house arrest or forced incarceration in psychiatric hospitals.[9]

So Howe would not have viewed himself as a hapless victim of political repression. He was well aware that other American intellectuals, artists, and entertainers—to cite just those in the world of American culture—were subject to far worse treatment than was he. Some of them lost their jobs as university professors or schoolteachers, others were blacklisted (e.g., as Hollywood screenwriters), and still others were harassed and summoned before HUAC to testify against former colleagues and friends (and in some cases were forbidden to travel or jailed on contempt charges for invoking the Fifth Amendment). By contrast, the periodic monitoring of Howe and his family represented an annoying pinprick, as he would have acknowledged. Although Howe's FBI file is far larger than that of either Trilling or Macdonald and the surveillance is clearly more intrusive and enduring, Howe's treatment by the FBI, even during the worst period under McCarthyism, produced no lasting or significant negative results for his personal or professional life. Instead, his career during the 1950s and 1960s advanced in a constant upward trajectory: his essays found their way into America's prominent mainstream magazines, his books appeared from the best publishing houses, his lack of a PhD proved no obstacle to professorships at prestigious universities (including Brandeis and Stanford), and *Dissent*'s circulation rose as its visibility widened.

As with Trilling and Macdonald, the FBI's pursuit of Howe is exemplary because of its needlessness, wastefulness, and maltreatment of an innocent American citizen who was simply voicing "dissent." Howe was doing so via platforms ranging from distinguished magazines such as *Partisan Review* and well-known New York publishing houses and was therefore attracting more notice and exerting more influence than most citizens. In principle, however, his activity was no different from theirs. The main difference was that his opinions were delivered in print from publications that were being discussed by interested and informed citizens throughout the nation.

LIFE OUTSIDE A SECT

The Bureau maintained an active file on Howe during 1951–59, including a Security Index on him in the Boston division. Howe's ethnic background may have been a factor—the Bureau pointedly noted that "his father, David [Horenstein], was born in Russia and was naturalized as a U.S. citizen in 1922, according to the records furnished by CCNY" (the City College of New York). The Russian birth might have indicated to the FBI a possible sympathy with communism.[10] But the specific occasion for the FBI file on Howe was the more aggressive use of the Smith Act in 1948–49 to prosecute radicals, which resulted in the conviction of several leading members of the American Communist Party (CPUSA) in October 1949. Passed in 1940, the Smith Act justified the scrutiny for national security reasons of all members of "basic revolutionary groups" committed to "the violent overthrow" of the U.S. government.

With the official support of the CPUSA, the Smith Act had first been used against the Left in 1941 to convict and jail SWP members, including its leader, James P. Cannon. In a letter to the Loyalty Review Board (September 29, 1949) contained in Howe's file, Attorney General J. Howard McGrath described the ISL as a "basic revolutionary group," the successor to the revolutionary Workers Party. Howe had belonged to the Workers Party since 1940 (and was a member of its national steering committee in 1946), and he had served as editor of the weekly *Labor Action*, the official organ of both the Workers Party and the ISL. (McGrath's letter specifically cited *Labor Action*.)[11]

Despite several background checks on Howe's agitprop activities in the 1940s, the FBI remained unaware that not long after entering the army, Howe resurfaced in both *Labor Action* and *New International* under the pseudonym R. Fahan, writing anti-war polemics. Especially after Trotsky's assassination in 1940, most American Trotskyists, including the Schachtmanites, took a strong position against the Second World War, condemning it as a battle among capitalist-imperialist powers, including the "state capitalism" of the Stalinist USSR. Howe's last wartime article appeared in October 1943. He did not return to the pages of *Labor Action* until February 11, 1946, usually thereafter writing as Irving Howe.[12] (The FBI apparently also did not know that Howe wrote under the name Theodore Dryden in 1947–48 for Dwight Macdonald's radical magazine, *politics*, or indeed that "subject Horenstein" was not "the father of two boys.")[13]

Typical of the FBI's lack of competence in its intelligence gathering on Howe is its close coverage of the circumstances of his departure from the ISL in October 1952.[14] Although the FBI file contains two copies of Howe's three-page resignation letter, Bureau informants seemed not to know about how complete the rupture was between Howe and the ISL. No mention is made in Howe's file of the ISL motion prohibiting its members from contributing articles to *Dissent* unless they received special dispensation. Throughout the 1950s, the FBI treated Howe as if he were still a member of a "basic revolutionary organization."

Nor was this the Bureau's only important oversight about Howe's political activities at this time. The Bureau apparently missed Howe's public dispute with the ISL two years later—his last contribution to *Labor Action*. In a scathing attack on the inaugural issue of *Dissent*, Hal Draper wrote in *Labor Action* on February 22, 1954, that Howe's break with the ISL and his founding of *Dissent* signified that "those who sympathize with his 'ethos' must likewise abandon any organized socialist movement, which is to be replaced by such a center for thinkers as his magazine seeks to make itself."

Howe replied to Draper in the March 15 issue of *Labor Action*: "I know [your] way of thinking, having suffered from it myself for a good many years." Howe maintained that Draper and the ISL were living in grandiose denial both about the reality of a socialist "movement" and about their influence beyond the suffocating *we* of their sectarian circle: "Life in a Sect" was the title Howe chose for the chapter devoted to his Trotskyist days in his memoir,

A Margin of Hope (1983). Although some individuals in America could still be called "socialists," Howe said, "we have no political significance, whatsoever."[15] Nonetheless, the Bureau worried in the early 1950s that socialists such as Howe might build a movement or gain political significance.

"AN IMMATURE OUTLOOK ON LIFE"

Howe's campus activities in the 1950s at Princeton, Brandeis, the University of Michigan, and elsewhere were also monitored periodically by regional FBI offices. When the FBI began its file on him in February 1951, Howe was living in Princeton, residing in a small house financed by a GI loan. His second wife, Thalia, taught Greek and Latin at Miss Fine's, a private day school in Princeton.[16] A colleague of hers who described herself as "casually acquainted with Irving Howe" provided Newark agents of the Bureau with some information in October 1953 about Howe's status as a full-time independent writer.

Another informant was Carlos Baker, a distinguished Hemingway scholar who taught at Princeton University. Baker was in the university audience when Howe lectured on the theme of "Politics and the Novel" at the Christian Gauss seminar in the fall of 1952. Baker was forty-three years old and had just published *Hemingway: The Writer as Artist*. A specialist in British and American literature who had been teaching since 1937 at Princeton, Baker was a rising academic star, soon to be appointed department chair. Baker was also well acquainted with the social milieu of the *PR* writers, a world Howe had just entered.

According to a September 22, 1952, report from the Newark bureau, Baker told the FBI that he knew "so little about the subject [that] he was in no position to provide any recommendations." On February 2, 1954, the agent added that Baker "did notice the subject has a very bright mind, a nervous disposition, and an immature outlook on life."

Although Baker evidently told FBI agents nothing of importance, their conversation with him indicates at minimum that he was willing to provide the Bureau with negative impressions of a young man whose background would certainly have been officially suspect. It also shows that the FBI gained access to prominent scholars familiar with Howe's intellectual life and reference groups. (Baker's name evidently appears in Howe's file because he died in 1987; the names of several other informants or agents, apparently all still alive when FOIA officials last reviewed the dossier, are blacked out.)[17]

In the fall of 1953, Howe joined the faculty at Brandeis University in Waltham, Massachusetts. (He would remain at Brandeis throughout the period of his

FBI file; he left for Stanford in 1961.) Within a few weeks, the Boston FBI office was following his activities. One report from the spring of 1954 reported on surveillance of his home in nearby Wellesley: "From January 16 to February 13, 1954, a mail cover was maintained on the residence of the subject at 87 Parker Road. The following are individuals or organizations with whom the subject received correspondence during this period: *Dissent*, *Perspectives*, [Stanley] Plastrik, *Partisan Review*." On June 2, Boston agents wrote, "Asked New York office to identify and check the references of some 15 correspondents of the subject. Because considerable agent time would be necessary to cover these leads, the New York office will not cover the leads as set out."

Surveillance of Howe intensified in 1954, perhaps because Brandeis was known as a home for numerous intellectual radicals and Marxists (and ex-Marxists). The timing may also have been triggered by the fact that in January 1954, Howe and his Brandeis colleague, Lewis Coser, joined forces as coeditors on the first issue of *Dissent*, whose name perfectly captured the stance that they and other contributors to the magazine adopted toward USSR and U.S. government policies, domestic as well as international. *Dissent* was vehemently anti-Stalinist and anti-Soviet, while a number of editorial board members, like Howe, were former Trotskyists or were refugee radicals with Western European backgrounds, like Coser.

Despite the aggressively anti-Soviet position of the *Dissent*ers—one of the distinguishing features of the group—most FBI agents were not skilled at drawing distinctions about left-wing affiliations among intellectuals. So there was often a tendency, as we have mentioned in previous chapters, to lump together various Trotskyist sects with Stalinist and other Marxist opponents as "Communists." The Marxist Left included many tiny splinter groups, a number of which were utterly hostile to the American Communist Party and the USSR. But few FBI agents understood the terrain of the balkanized American Left, and for some of their informants (as was the case for Trilling and Macdonald) it was also terra incognita.

Other factors probably also influenced the FBI's decision to move more aggressively on Howe. For instance, word was obviously spreading in mainstream culture about Howe's growing stature as an intellectual and activist. (Brandeis president Abram Sachar apparently regarded Howe's appointment in 1953 as "a major coup," at least in hindsight.)[18] Moreover, Howe was soon to become a well-known campus presence at Brandeis because of his frequent participation in public debates, including face-offs with such figures as Herbert Marcuse, the Stalinist novelist Howard Fast, and Oscar Handlin (who debated Howe on Israel's capture and planned trial of Adolf Eichmann).

Irving Howe with his son, Nicholas, and daughter, Nina, in 1954, when the family lived in Wellesley, Massachusetts.

Courtesy: Nina Howe

The Boston FBI tracked down "subject Horenstein" for an interview in August 1954, near the Harvard campus.[19] The August 26 report of the interview began,

The Boston office interviewed subject Horenstein without prior notice at 2:00 p.m., August 6, 1954 by two Special Agents, on Boylston Street, Cambridge, Massachusetts. Subject was affable. He stated he would be happy to sit in his own car and discuss ideologies. He continued that this was as far as he would go with the interviewing agents and that he had no intention of identifying or "involving" others in view of what he described as the "misuse" of the Smith Act by the Department of Justice and the use of Executive Order 10450 to "blackball radicals and prevent them from earning a livelihood." It is to be noted that at no time during the course of the interview was the subject hostile, and throughout the interview he displayed a friendly and cordial manner.

According to the report, "Subject described himself as a 'Socialist' and a lifelong 'anti-Stalinist.' Subject denied membership at any time in the Socialist Workers Party or any other group or organization which advocates the overthrow of the United States government by force or violence." Finally, the report concluded, "In view of the subject's past activities and attitude at the time of interview and his denial of membership in the Socialist Workers Party, it is believed that he should be included in the security index." The Security Index card was prepared on the same day as the report.

This interview forms the centerpiece of the comprehensive file on Howe compiled by the Boston office on April 8, 1955. That file comprises twenty-six pages, including birth records, educational background, marital status, military service record, employment record, residences, political activities, speeches and writings, and even speeding tickets in Princeton and nearby Cranbury, New Jersey ("ten dollars paid on February 8, 1953, seven dollars paid on 3/23/53"). The April 1955 file also includes Howe's resignation letter to the ISL, a log of his contributions to the *New International* between 1946 and 1952, and a summary of three of his fall 1949 public lectures, which reflected the themes of his book, *The U.A.W. and Walter Reuther*, and coincided with its publication.[20]

CLOSING THE FILE

Several regional bureaus intermittently followed Howe's activities during the late 1950s, but he was no longer considered a security risk after mid-1955, and little new information appeared in his file as the decade wound down.

On May 19, 1955, the Boston office decided to cancel the Security Index. However, it sought to justify its expenditure of resources, noting yet again that "the subject registered with the Worker's Party in June/July, 1946 at which time he indicated he had been a member of the Worker's Party since 1940." The four-page report closes, "While the subject has been a member of a basic revolutionary group within the past five years, it is noted that on October 12, 1952, subject directed a letter to the ISL in which he stated he was formally resigning from the ISL, further it is noted that subject has stated that in the event of hostilities with the Soviet Union, the ISL should support the United States. It is, therefore, recommended that he be removed from the Security Index. The security flash note is also to be removed." This report was filed on June 10, 1955.

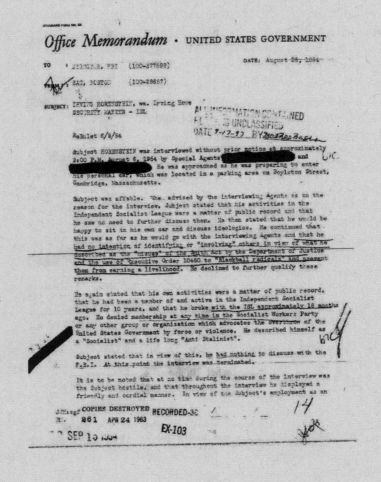

Irving Howe (aka Horenstein) was stopped and accosted in August 1954, after he founded *Dissent*, which billed itself as a "socialist quarterly." The FBI decided to escalate its surveillance of Howe and make "Horenstein" the subject of a Security Index Card. The FBI "interview was conducted in a particularly circumspect manner," the report noted, yet this occurred not because the Bureau sought to protect the Howe family's privacy or Howe's reputation in the community but instead "in order that no embarrassment to the Bureau would result."

Nonetheless, the Boston office still conducted occasional spot checks of Howe. His file reports a "pretext telephone call to Brandeis University on 10/30/58, in the guise of an associate attempting to locate subject."[21] Boston agents also tipped off other regional bureaus about Howe's whereabouts and coordinated surveillance with them. The Detroit file for March 31, 1959, notes that on October 18, 1958, Howe "directed a postcard to *Labor Action*," requesting a change of address for his subscription. Indeed, the March Detroit file is a twenty-two-page report, including a substantial nine-page appendix on Howe's memberships in various socialist organizations.

Howe's third wife, Arien Hausknecht, taught at the University of Michigan at Ann Arbor during part of his leave of absence from Brandeis in 1958–59. The Detroit FBI checked up on him in Ann Arbor and also noted that he was "employed at Wayne State University in the English department on a part-time basis."[22]

Detroit agents attended at least three of Howe's *Dissent* talks during 1956–58. (Much of Howe's energy in the late 1950s went into organizing *Dissent* forums around the country on various political topics, an effort that did not go unnoticed by the FBI.)[23] One informant at a Detroit talk reported that the

> principal subject of Howe's talk was how sorry he was to have ever considered himself as a "socialist" and that if he had to do it over again, he would not associate himself with such a movement because he felt that it would never amount to much more than just a movement. Howe further stated that, in spite of its ideals and some of the fanatics [who] are members of various socialists' [*sic*] organizations, there is no real socialist movement. Howe, during his talk, referred to *Dissent* magazine and its program and stated that the magazine staff had considered dropping the word "social" or "socialist" from its program, but had finally decided not to make any change.

This informant was doubtless confusing *socialist* and *Trotskyist*, failing to grasp that Howe was referring to his years of membership in the ISL. Even if internal discussions on the *Dissent* editorial board considered abandoning a formal commitment to "socialism," Howe proudly and publicly referred to himself as a socialist throughout the 1950s and well after. Howe's self-professed socialism notwithstanding, however, his overall political outlook had further moderated by the late 1950s, evolving away from a radical politics and toward a firm liberal anti-communism and radical humanism.[24] Howe's anti-Stalinist stance never wavered, but his "socialism" became less an active political engagement and more (as Draper had predicted in 1954) an ethos or axiology, a commitment to what Howe himself in *Dissent* called "the animating ethic of socialism."[25]

To sustain and fortify that commitment, Howe looked for and wrote about European socialists such as Hungarian György Konrád and the Italian Ignazio Silone, both of whom he embraced as inspirational presences. From the mid-1950s onward, Silone was in fact Howe's most cherished model of radical commitment, the living figure above all others whom Howe exalted as a socialist exemplar for both himself and *Dissent* readers.[26]

Like the Detroit FBI, Boston agents were also concerned that *Dissent*'s public forums might lead to a socialist mass movement.[27] (A 1959 forum that featured Erich Fromm, a *Dissent* editorial board member, drew seven hundred people.)[28] For instance, the Boston office reported on "Irving Horenstein" at a *Dissent* forum on "The Revolt in East Europe" (December 1, 1956) at Adelphi Hall in New York and a forum in Boston (January 30, 1957) attended by a lieutenant of the Massachusetts State Police. According to the report of the New York talk, which dealt with the Soviet invasion of Hungary in October 1956, Howe "definitely was anti-Communist in his analysis and repeatedly criticized the ruthless attacks by the Russian troops."[29]

According to an April 4, 1958, report on another *Dissent* forum covered by the Boston office, Howe "evidenced considerable dejection over the low level of activity that now characterized U.S. socialism." The file continues, "Howe claims that socialism could meet all the problems that besetted [*sic*] in our country if trends were to continue unchanged. As he saw them, there would probably result in our country a low-charged autocracy, somewhere between freedom and totalitarianism. Howe stated that in central planning even of the socialist variety, there was a danger that the concentration of powerful planning purposes would destroy freedom and to be successful and accepted, U.S. socialism must be democratic and welcome some degree of small independent business. Howe concluded with a plea for studied regroupment of socialist elements."

By this time, the FBI had in effect acknowledged that Howe was no "security risk." But the Bureau's reclassification was evidently influenced by new legislative constraints, too. The reduced scope permitted to the FBI by judicial decisions following the discrediting of Senator Joseph McCarthy's witch hunts also limited its pursuit of young ex-Trotskyists like Howe. Indeed, an important reason for the Bureau's dwindling interest in Howe, along with many other former "revolutionaries," was that the U.S. Supreme Court had recently defined the Smith Act more narrowly. In 1957, the Supreme Court had ruled on a California case (*Yates v. United States*), saying that to win a conviction, prosecutors must demonstrate a "clear and present danger." The Supreme Court thereby sharply curbed the application of the Smith Act, allowing it to pertain only to people who engaged in specific insurrectionist activities

Irving Howe with his daughter, Nina, 1958, when
the family resided in Belmont, Massachusetts.

Courtesy: Nina Howe

or incited others to do so.[30] These developments rendered "Horenstein"—a
third-rank former "revolutionary" from a negligible sect—of little interest.[31]

LESS FREE = MORE SECURE?

Does the treatment of Irving Howe during the McCarthy era hold any lessons for us today? Yes. It serves as a cautionary reminder that we may adopt
draconian and obsessive security measures that will comfort all alarmists—
but the consequence is that we will become less free, not safer. Less free, not

more secure. Such interference with our civil liberties is also an assault on the Constitution and the Bill of Rights.

Let us transcend the pseudo-patriotic jingoism that makes us either "100 percent American" or "Un-American."

Let us question the crude dichotomies common to both the Red Scare and the September 11 decade that make one either with the United States or with the commies and terrorists, respectively.

Let us work together, in a spirit of mutual respect for differences of opinion, to forge a balance between enlightened authority and responsible dissent.

EPILOGUE
THE ORWELLIAN FUTURE?

Everybody knows that corruption thrives in secret places,
and avoids public places, and we believe it a fair presumption
that secrecy means impropriety. . . . Let there be light!
—Woodrow Wilson, 1912

We seek a free flow of information across national boundaries
and oceans, across iron curtains and stone walls. We are not
afraid to entrust the American people with unpleasant facts,
foreign ideas, alien philosophies, and competitive values.
—John F. Kennedy, 1962

A fellow *Partisan Review* contributor, regarded as a kind of intellectual "big brother" by all four of the New York Intellectuals discussed in this study, hovers over these pages.[1] George Orwell, the first recipient (in 1949) of the Partisan Review Award for distinguished writing, was also a prominent cultural and social critic whose personal life and written work attracted the attention of the intelligence services in Britain, the United States, and elsewhere, especially after his death.[2] His final masterwork, *Nineteen Eighty-Four*, as everyone knows, features a horrific and tyrannical dictator, Big Brother, whom Orwell imagined as a Janus-faced totalitarian bogeyman figure, a hideous and fearful caricature of Hitler and Stalin merged into one. Utterly nightmarish is the evil superstate, Oceania, which effectively propagandizes more than 90 percent of the population to believe that they face the prospect of annihilation alternately from the superstates of Eurasia and Eastasia. Big Brother is an invisible, apparently mythic, presence throughout the novel, striking terror in the hearts of the populace to the extent that they essentially become willing zombies who give up their civil liberties in exchange for state protection.

Nineteen Eighty-Four is a satirical anti-utopia and a projection of what Orwell feared the Western democracies could become in his time. And what about in our time, more than three full decades beyond his novel's title year, which the post-war zeitgeist—in an incomparable feat of negative branding—has forever darkened?

WARFARE, FROM COLD TO CYBER?

The Cold War has passed, but the cyberwars are upon us. (Are "Star Wars" far behind?) The post-communist New World Order of the twenty-first century has already witnessed "Orwellian" developments—rogue states, drones, government-sponsored cyberattacks, and on and on—that make the bugaboos of midcentury seem by comparison as medieval as the rack and dungeon. The specter of terrorism and its offshoots, along with the far-reaching, digitized tentacles of both government and private industry, imperil our right to privacy and freedom of expression far more pervasively and insidiously than the thuggish hardware of the past. Not to mention today's sophisticated psychoterror: old-fashioned physical torture has been supplemented and extended through "enhanced interrogation techniques"—a Newspeak locution for waterboarding, mock executions, "deep cold" exposure, "rectal rehydration," nakedness in total darkness and isolation, and shell-game-type "extraordinary rendition" (i.e., transportation to a succession of secret "black-site" prisons).

During the McCarthy and the Stalinist eras, such things were the stuff of dystopian fiction. Nowadays—as in Room 101—"they" *can* "get inside you." Mutatis mutandis, the so-called Free World faces "totalitarian" threats formerly unknown—and almost unimagined except in Orwellian horror scenarios. Yet fiction is fast approaching fact, leaving many of us feeling less free *and* less secure than ever before.

Will our technology outflank our technical capacity—and our moral will—to safeguard civil liberties? The danger is there.

Yes, Big Brother is watching us. Yet do we not collude in our insecurities—and our unfreedoms? The seductive Baconian proclamation "Knowledge Is Power" mesmerizes us with its macho promise that Mother Earth is ours to dominate. Instead, however, as we succumb to this sadistic lure of technological omnipotence, our glistering hardware and magical software entrance us like a spellbinding utopian dream. Our Eden with its shiny Apple! Ever greater scope and speed—ever more Power!—at the mere cost of a click. Our power lust proves insatiable—and disempowering. As we embrace the Faustian bargain, our miraculous gadgetry processes and perverts us into obsessive control freaks. Cozily ensconced inside the Matrix, we too, like Oceania's zombie-like proles, reflexively surrender our leisure, our health, our social lives, and our physical senses to the hypnotic screen. The (virtual) reality today is that the dream has turned nightmarish, whereby "Knowledge Is Power" inverts into the culminating, worshipful chant to Big Brother: "*Ignorance Is Strength!*"[3]

Beyond the "conventional" (or neoconventional) terrorists facing us, Orwellian forecasters surveying the cyberscape fret about the ever more imaginable nightmare of possible cyberwar, a battle distinguished by warhead-type code or digital worms deployed to decimate infrastructure and even murder human beings.[4] These mega-viruses infect rival networks, causing them to self-destruct or implode/explode. Orwellian voices argue that a cyber arms race is well under way. Michael Hayden, a former director of the Central Intelligence Agency (CIA) and the National Security Agency (NSA), has characterized such code as "a new class of weapon, a weapon never before used," that possesses the "whiff of August, 1945."[5] The only question is whether this future conflict will be "hot" or "cold." Will it be Cyber World War III or the Cyber Cold War? One expert has predicted that it will be a "cool war"—"a little warmer than cold because it seems likely to involve almost constant offensive measures that, while falling short of actual warfare, regularly seek to damage or weaken rivals or gain an edge through violations of sovereignty and penetration of defenses."[6]

Of course, in one key respect, cyberwarfare is utterly unlike conventional terrorism. Cyberthreats are invisible and surreptitious, whereas terrorist groups such as ISIS thrive on sensation and spectacle. And yet, as President Barack Obama has acknowledged, both kinds of terrorism, whether in the form of endless rendition and physical torture or of drone strikes and surgical cyberattacks, "raise difficult questions about the balance we strike between our interest in security and our values of privacy."[7] Since 9/11, the "balance" arguably still falls heavily on the side of limiting liberty in the name of security. Numerous critics contend in fact that the differences between the Bush and Obama administrations on national security are chiefly rhetorical, leading *The Economist* to dub Obama "W's Apprentice."[8] Other observers brand him "Big Brother Obama" and proclaim mockingly, "Yes We Scan" (a derisive pun on his popular 2008 campaign slogan, "Yes We Can").[9]

Given the current state of affairs, in which incursions into, even abrogations of, our personal freedoms are so ubiquitous as to render them a casual, matter-of-fact norm of contemporary life, I believe that Orwell would voice anew his anxieties of yesteryear. Whether applied to state torture or technotrespass, his novel's cautionary warnings are unfortunately evergreen.[10]

Warnings? I conceded in the Prologue that history yields no explicit lessons. That applies equally or even more to serious fiction.

Maybe "*unlessons*"?

If so, one germane and cautionary *unlesson* in *Nineteen Eighty-Four* is that a visible external threat—such as both Eurasia and Eastasia represent for Oceania, or which Emanuel Goldstein's dissident underground "Brotherhood" signified for the Inner Party—makes it much easier to achieve national unity and consensus on geopolitical goals. For decades, the bête noire of communism (especially the so-called Red Fascism of Stalin's rule) served the West well in this regard. In fact, it served so well that the West—the purported Cold War victor—seemed rather disoriented or even demoralized by the "victory" in 1989–91. Our leaders could not forge consensus and cohesion in the absence of a common enemy. In a certain sense, peacetime was more difficult than wartime in the 1990s, putting a new twist on the Oceania slogan "*War Is Peace*." "Islamicism" (an *ism* designed to distinguish terrorist activity from Islam) and al-Qaeda/ISIS/IS have served partially since the disappearance of the USSR in 1991 as substitute bogeymen, though Vladimir Putin and Russia are undeniably making a comeback as contenders for that dubious distinction.

Can we not do without an enemy scapegoat? For all his hatred of Stalinism, Orwell did not regard "U-S-S-R" as some kind of Hate Weak rallying cry for the West. In his essays of the 1940s on James Burnham's *The Managerial Revolution* and *The Struggle for the World*, Orwell argued that the ex-Communist Burnham, a belligerent anti-Stalinist, exaggerated the durability and might of Stalin's tyrannical regime. In doing so, Burnham overemphasized the likelihood that a bureaucratic-technocratic elite of party functionaries would arise and furnish both dynastic stability and quasi-permanence to one-party dictatorships in totalitarian states.

I suspect that Orwell would also have voiced skepticism about Burnham's campaign of the 1950s, along with those of Republican leaders such as John Foster Dulles, for an "offensive" strategy aimed at reversing the territorial gains of Soviet communism—even if "rollback" meant dropping a nuclear bomb.[11] Much as Orwell deplored the "evil empires" of Oceania, Eurasia, and Eastasia in *Nineteen Eighty-Four*, a stalemate prevails in the novel after the nuclear wars of the 1950s—probably a reflection of Orwell's pragmatic preference for an enduring Cold War rather than the confrontational stance urged by Dulles, who declared in 1952 that the United States must abandon "treadmill policies" and adopt "aggressive" tactics.[12]

By implication, Orwell broadly shared the outlook that guided the main architects of American post-war diplomacy during the Cold War: containment. Orwell's geopolitical worldview resembled George Kennan's in this crucial respect: Orwell too was a "realist."[13] He was a rebel and a gradualist, not a fundamentalist ideologue and revolutionary. As R. J. Stove has pointed out,

> Before the Spanish Popular Front, [Orwell] sought no democratic crusades inside or outside Europe. He never called for an invasion of, or even sanctions against, Mussolini's Italy. Of non-Italian and non-Nazi rightist dictators, he abhorred Franco alone. If he ever denounced Chancellor Dollfuss, General Metaxas, or Admiral Horthy, it has escaped his editors. Toward Marshal Pétain and Pilsudski he showed subdued aversion rather than loud anger. (He made one neutral reference, in 1944, to Dr Salazar's rule of Portugal.) . . . Also, he resented those Zionists who blew up the King David Hotel.[14]

Orwell's realism made him skeptical about bellicose initiatives for "regime change" or indeed the kind of adventurism that would be involved in (re)making the world safe for democracy. Nor did he advocate deploying the atom bomb to roll back the Soviet army from occupied Eastern Europe or argue that first-strike capability in atomic or nuclear weaponry—let alone a mutually assured destruction policy—was essential. Instead, he took a pragmatic view that, with qualifications and ambivalences, clearly sided with America and a version of realpolitik. Given Orwell's refusal to support aggressive military options in the Cold War, it seems most unlikely that he would have sanctioned such responses in a (still comparatively) lesser conflict such as the War on Terror.

Orwell certainly also retained a sense of historical scale, whereby he recognized that a politics of equivalence was, as it were, spatial presentism. And it was no less misconceived. Distinctions—both political and historical—need to be drawn. To equate McCarthyism (or what Orwell called "one hundred percent Americanism") with Stalinism—or for that matter, East German "Stasi-ism" with Nazism—elides the distinctions within each pair.[15] We, too, need to maintain such balance, which includes the judicious use of political and historical analogies. That is to say, equating the War on Terror with the Cold War is also misconceived. No "Big Brother" totalitarianisms exist on the globe today. Even North Korea is at worst an example of "Little Brother." Equating the terrorists of today with the totalitarian regimes of the last century diminishes the historical experience of the Cold War, let alone World War II. For example, the all-too-casual comparisons between murderous Islamist terrorist cells and Bolshevik genocide—the latter a "democide" accounting for one hundred million twentieth-century corpses—insult the victims of the latter.

Despite these significant differences between totalitarian nation-states and terrorist networks, however, might the vision and views of Orwell the Cold Warrior still speak to our present circumstances? Might the "realist" sensibility of Orwell's anti-utopia and anti-Burnham essays possess practical contemporary relevance? That is to say, might some version of Cold War containment serve American policymakers today with a cogent strategy—absent any recourse to fundamentalist theology—for a patient, long-term anti-terrorist campaign on multiple fronts?[16] Like Soviet communism with its fatal self-contradictions, might "Islamicist" terrorism eventually implode? Could the West "contain" international terrorism with limited measures in the long term without recourse to large-scale military operations, monitoring it loosely in the conviction that it will subvert itself?

WATCHING BIG BROTHER WATCHING US

Whether or not such a "containment" strategy could succeed—or even gain support as a new Western consensus—concerned citizens need to practice a constant form of "containment" of our own. *We* need to keep watching Big Brother, ever on the alert for abuses by our own government and our own geopolitical side. Yes, we need to keep watching Big Brother even as he (or it) watches us. We need to keep our eyes on *them* as they keep their telescreen eye on us. If we value the freedoms that represent the cornerstone of a democracy, watching Big Brother is indispensable to exposing the perils to freedom and privacy before we lose them.

The ultimate *un*lesson of Cold War surveillance excesses in general and of *Nineteen Eighty-Four* in particular is a stern and challenging one. It comes down to this: the best means to combat those forces that would conspire to destroy our liberties is to refuse to curtail them in the name of national security. Rather, it is to champion humane values as the proper counterforce.

In addition, we must also insist that these values be maintained and defended even in the face of sadistic acts of mass violence; indeed, we must hold firm to the position that those who cherish democracy will not sacrifice the fundamental principles on which both our civic integrity as a nation and our basic human dignity rest.

ACKNOWLEDGMENTS

The origins of his book lie more than four decades in the past. During the late 1960s and early 1970s, I watched Efrem Zimbalist Jr. in the hit TV series *The F.B.I.* Zimbalist played the role of Inspector Lewis Erskine, an impeccably dressed, engaging, and thoroughly likable agent who never seemed to fail. If you were "wanted by the FBI," it was just a matter of time before your time was up. (I later discovered that Zimbalist was personally quite friendly with J. Edgar Hoover, who treated the series as a public relations vehicle and—with the full cooperation of the show's producers—conducted background checks on all actors who played FBI agents.)

Entering high school, I began to read press reports of wiretapping and bugging by the U.S. intelligence agencies, along with investigative stories by Drew Pearson and Jack Anderson, who were syndicated columnists in our local paper. I was a staffer on my high school newspaper and active on the speech and debate team. As a fourteen-year-old, I wrote a speech entitled "Big Brotherhood, 1972"—unearthed decades later by my parents—in which I earnestly contended that America was heading down the path of Orwell's *Nineteen Eighty-Four*. One passage admonished,

> Grave threats, today more than ever before, are posed to the right to be alone—the right to privacy—by telephonic surveillance, or wiretapping, and electronic surveillance, or bugging.
>
> But, you may wonder, why shouldn't our government wiretap and bug suspected criminals who may be breaking the law by murdering, kidnapping, plotting against our government, or any number of other offenses? After all, the underworld isn't ethical, is it? Shouldn't we fight fire with fire?"

The answer to these questions must be no. Those who claim to fight injustice's cause must not lose sight of the fact that in the fervent pursuit of criminals, privacy must be preserved. No justice is achieved when one crime is solved by another. When the government employs criminal methods, it is no more law-abiding than the so-called criminal himself.

I subsequently received three phone calls from FBI agents inquiring about my speech, which I had delivered in various local competitions in high school forensics. Did some dastardly informant, disguised as a forensics coach from a rival school—or heavens, a fellow student!—report on me?

I doubt it. I had ingenuously written to the FBI requesting information to support or rebut my speech, and it is more likely that several months later, some agent had gotten around to reading the letter. I mentioned my research, including references to former attorney general Ramsey Clark and other critics of the U.S. intelligence community, who were making headlines with claims about the government's infringements on civil rights in the name of national security.

All this occurred in the wake of the Safe Streets and Crime Control Act of 1968, which Clark and my watchdog columnists castigated. My speech cited their evidence that this legislation contained many loopholes that allowed government agencies to wiretap and bug, with little real oversight. I remember one FBI agent questioning me about the following passage in my speech:

> Not only are wiretaps and bugs invasions of privacy, but in reality they are often ineffective and inefficient. For what little surveillance accomplishes, it is a waste of law enforcement time and money. The fact that science has developed a dangerous instrument does not mean that mankind must employ it. Science has created the atom bomb. I propose that we exercise the same caution with regard to wiretaps and bugs [as] in the case of the atom bomb.
>
> If we fail to do this, our society may reach "1984" well before we reach that year. Only if society insists on it today will privacy—the right to be let alone—exist in its true form tomorrow.

As the widespread fears since 9/11 about the restriction of civil liberties and the expansion of police power and government surveillance demonstrate, the warnings in *Nineteen Eighty-Four* (and my little speech!) haven't lost their relevance.

Yes, the child is father to the man. Government surveillance, Cold War politics—and even George Orwell, *NEF*, and Big Brother. It's all there—and now it's here in this book.

So let me first thank my unforgettable high school forensics teacher, John Buettler, for patiently guiding that nervy young man of yesteryear through several revisions of his speech. We have remained close friends through the years, and I am the proud godfather of one of John's children, who is now an adult nearing the age of forty.

My other debts are more recent yet no less heartfelt. I thank Edward Alexander, Gorman Beauchamp, Daniel Connell, Maurice duQuesnay, Ethan Goffman, Eugene Goodheart, Michael Kazin, Michael Levenson, Steve Longstaff, Jack Rossi, Jim Sleeper, and Stephen Whitfield for their conversations about the *Partisan Review* writers in general or this study in particular. I am especially grateful to Morris Dickstein and Alan Wald, who encouraged this book from its inception a decade ago and with whom I have discussed its direction and details.

My last and deepest thanks go to Alan Munton, my beneficent big brother, who read every line with care and made numerous valuable suggestions. Like me, Alan is a student of British literature and a strong admirer of George Orwell. He is also an erudite scholar of the modernist literary movement in twentieth-century European art and letters, above all the work of Wyndham Lewis. It is my blessed good fortune that Alan is not only a generous friend and convivial comrade but also a gifted editor who possesses an encyclopedic mind and an uncanny talent for spotting errors of usage and misinterpretations of evidence. It has been both a pleasure and honor to get to know him better through working with him on this book.

For all these reasons and more, I dedicate this study to Alan.

NOTES

As indicated in the notes below, selective use has been made of the Michael Josselson Papers and the Nicolas Nabokov Papers, both of which contain unpublished material pertinent to this study. These collections are archived at the Harry Ransom Center at the University of Texas at Austin, and I have cited them according to box and folder numbers. (Josselson and Nabokov were officers of the Paris-based Congress for Cultural Freedom. Both men were officially—and secretly—employed by the CIA.) Declassified government letters and memorandums from the 1940s through 1970s that bear on the themes of this book and pertain to the lives and careers of the *PR* writers discussed in the book are also included here. Assembled into government dossiers that often totaled several hundred pages of documents, these files amassed by the U.S. government were released to me through the Freedom of Information Act. Whenever possible, I have identified them by their date and Bureau file (Bufile) number.

PREFACE

1. See John Rodden, *The Intellectual Species: Evolution or Extinction?* (London: Troubador, 2017).

PROLOGUE: THE TRADITION OF THE NEW

1. See, for example, Derek Chollet and James Goldgeier, *America between the Wars: From 11/9 to 9/11: The Misunderstood Years between the Fall of the Berlin Wall and the Start of the War on Terror* (New York: Public Affairs, 2008). Chilean director Mel Chin's animated film, *9-11/11-9*, has also publicized the connections between the two dates; the film won several international awards.

2. The now-famous phrase owes to the influence of Samuel P. Huntington's *The Clash of Civilizations and the Remaking of the World Order* (New York: Simon and Schuster, 1996). Huntington contended that the "new world" of the post–Cold War period had witnessed the end of the "age of ideology." Henceforth the axis of conflict would be along cultural and religious lines, ultimately embodied in the form of a clash between civilizations.

3. The association between November 1989 and "The End of History" results from Francis Fukuyama's essay by that title in *The National Interest*, a journal of international affairs. Fukuyama appended a question mark to his title, but his postmodernist argument was that the collapse of communism in East Germany—and the full-scale discrediting of state socialism throughout Eastern Europe (and the USSR)—represented not just the end of the Cold War or even the era of socialism since the Bolshevik Revolution of 1917. Rather, in opposition to Marx, Western liberal democracy—not communism and the dictatorship of the proletariat—represented the "endpoint" of history. According to Fukuyama, no further large-scale structural changes in either systems of government or economics would hereafter occur. Fukuyama later expanded the essay into *The End of History and the Last Man* (New York: Free Press, 1992).

Huntington's work was conceived in reply to Fukuyama. Huntington maintained that the conflict between ideologies in recent centuries was a temporary phenomenon that had indeed run its course but that Fukuyama had erred in viewing that conflict as fundamental or its passing as "the end of history." On the contrary, contended Huntington, the conflict between ideologies was giving way to the ancient "core" clash between religions and cultures (or "civilizations").

4. The phrase "New World Order" first gained widespread currency at the end of World War I through Woodrow Wilson's Fourteen Points, in which he used the term to project a vision of a peaceful world arbitrated by a League of Nations. The phrase was relaunched at the close of the Cold War, when Presidents Mikhail Gorbachev and George H. W. Bush used it, albeit differently. Gorbachev spoke of a post–Cold War age of cooperation between the great powers of the East and West. Bush's accent was more unilateral, emphasizing a world in which the United States had become the sole superpower and thus had virtually uncontested authority to lead the world.

5. "Year Zero" derived from a popular German phrase, *Stunde Null* (Zero Hour), which referred to the Germans' hope that 1945 was not a year of disastrous defeat but rather an epochal moment for a *Neubeginn*. The English-language phrase is also associated with the widely popular book by Ian Buruma, *Year Zero: A History of 1945* (London: Penguin, 2013).

6. Recalling the ebullient American mood in mid-1945, William Barrett remembered a conversation in which his friend and fellow *Partisan Review* assistant editor Delmore Schwartz kept repeating, "1919! 1919! It's 1919 over again." Barrett continued, "History never repeats itself, they say, but in this case, in this new post-war world of ours, it might repeat the pattern if not the detail. Surely some splendid and flourishing period lay before us even if we could not foresee what it would be like" (*The Truants: Adventures among the Intellectuals* [New York: Anchor/Doubleday, 1982], 32).

For Barrett, Schwartz, and the other *Partisan Review* writers, the chant was "1945! 1945! It's 1945!" And in this respect, paradoxically, they believed that history was repeating itself insofar as it was "starting over again." Their feeling was that of a hopeful young generation before whom lay a seemingly limitless future of untold possibilities.

7. I borrow here for my own purposes the book title of a *Partisan Review* colleague and fellow member of the senior generation of New York Intellectuals, Harold Rosenberg, who wrote *The Tradition of the New* (New York: Horizon, 1959). Rosenberg was an art critic–historian, and the book discusses the post–World War II New York art scene in general and developments such as action painting in particular.

8. As the Cold War still raged, Harry Howe Ransom, among the first analysts of U.S. intelligence agencies, published *Can American Democracy Survive Cold War?* (New York: Doubleday, 1963). He sounded an alarm that this study recalibrates for the digital age: "The existence of a large, secret bureaucracy [that is] sometimes pivotally important in making and implementing national policies and strategies raises special problems" (173). Ransom focused on the Central Intelligence Agency, but his book possessed wide scope, and his warnings about the perils of secrecy for a democracy applied to all agencies in the intelligence community: the twin dangers of invisible government and of a tyrannical, arbitrary ("secret") police.

9. On the use and abuse of historical and political analogies, see the Epilogue.

10. Eric Goldman, *The Crucial Decade—And After: America, 1945–1960* (New York: Vintage, 1960).

11. Despite such headline-grabbing revelations as the alleged tapping of the mobile phones of more than three dozen world leaders, spying—even between close allies—is nothing new. The publicity accorded to Snowden's revelations derives less from new information released than from the documented confirmation they have provided about Washington's domestic and foreign surveillance practices.

Many critics, however, regard the former NSA contractor as a traitor for his "theft" of documents that contain little about domestic surveillance or the transgression of civil liberties. Instead, the vast majority of the leaked documents discuss secret espionage operations against the cybercapabilities of adversaries. For example, Left-liberal Senator Dianne Feinstein (D., Calif.), head of the Senate Intelligence Committee, labeled Snowden's release of classified documents "an act of treason" (Jeremy Herb and Justin Sink, "Sen. Feinstein Calls Snowden's NSA Leaks an 'Act of Treason,'" *The Hill*, June 10, 2013, http://thehill.com/policy/defense/304573-sen-feinstein-snowdens-leaks-are-treason).

At issue are the contents of 1.7 million documents that Snowden copied from more than two dozen top secret storage compartments in computers at the Signals Intelligence Center in Hawaii. In June 2013 he released some of this material to reporters, such as those at the *Guardian* in London, who published them to international indignation and acclaim, earning the newspapers and their reporters Pulitzer and other journalistic prizes. See, for example, Edward Jay Epstein, "Was Snowden's Heist a Foreign Operation?" *Wall Street Journal*, May 9, 2014.

12. In December 2013 federal judge Richard J. Leon called the National Security

Agency's policy of phone data collection "almost Orwellian," and concluded, "It is one thing to say that people expect phone companies to occasionally provide information to law enforcement. It is quite another that our citizens expect all phone companies to operate what is effectively a joint intelligence-gathering operation with the government" (Maureen Dowd, "Spying Run Amok," *New York Times*, December 18, 2013).

Anticipating my turn in the Epilogue to an extended consideration of the contemporary relevance of *Nineteen Eighty-Four* and the "Orwellian" aspects of the postmodern "surveillance state," it is inviting to ask whether Edward Snowden sees himself as a victimized Winston Smith. Would George Orwell, an unabashed Cold Warrior who handed his private list of suspected Communists to the Information Research Department, Britain's early post-war analogue to the Central Intelligence Agency, have derided Snowden as a post-9/11 quisling? Or would the Orwell who hated Empire, championed "Freedom of the Press" (in his essay of that title), and suffered official censorship (Churchill personally nixed Orwell's prospects of becoming a wartime correspondent in India) have celebrated Snowden as a freedom fighter? Or, for that matter, how would the New York Intellectuals profiled in the study have judged Snowden's actions in the post–Cold War context of Islamic radicals' war on the West? And the West's responses, ranging from drone attacks abroad to stepped-up surveillance at home? Would they regard him as a whistleblowing hero or criminal? As another Alger Hiss cum Julius Rosenberg? Or as another Daniel Ellsberg? (Ellsberg himself has defended Snowden.) Impossible to answer—if intriguing (and potentially insightful) to ask. And also dangerous if, as I underscore in the Epilogue, distinctions and details borne of patient reflection are not honored.

CHAPTER ONE. INTELLECTUALS AND INTELLIGENCE SERVICES: THE *PARTISAN REVIEW* WRITERS UNDER THE WATCHFUL EYE OF THE FBI

1. That phrase refers to Hannah Arendt's *Eichmann in Jerusalem: A Report on the Banality of Evil* (New York: Viking, 1963), her report and analysis of the trial in Israel of former Nazi leader Adolf Eichmann. Arendt was another leading member of the senior generation of the New York Intellectuals, though she was often regarded as an outsider because of her late arrival in the 1940s as a refugee from Nazi Germany, and her book generated controversy by claiming that European Jews collaborated in their own destruction during the Holocaust.

Dwight Macdonald played a cameo role in the Eichmann controversy in 1963–64. Adopting a stance that both set him further apart from his *PR* colleagues and demonstrated his inveterate inclination to go against the grain of his reference group, Macdonald belonged to the minority of Arendt's supporters, such as Mary McCarthy, who defended *Eichmann in Jerusalem*. The book triggered fierce exchanges and mutual recrimination from its critics and advocates within the New York Jewish community. Macdonald was a close friend of Arendt, and he respected her as a fellow cosmopolitan who disavowed the ethnic partisanship of her Jewish intellectual critics. Macdonald admired Arendt for maintaining an allegiance to independent, internationalist values that opposed patriotism and jingoism of all types. (Macdonald was an anti-Zionist because of his anti-statist, anarchistic convictions.)

2. Thomas Kuhn, *The Structure of Scientific Revolutions* (Chicago: University of Chicago Press, 1996). In Kuhn's now-classic distinction, "normal science" is "standard operating procedure." Such research proceeds "within the existing paradigm" that follows scientific method and aims to confirm/refute established results. By contrast, "revolutionary science" shifts the paradigm, introducing a new world view. Revolutionary shifts rarely occur. Einstein's quantum mechanics, which revolutionized Newtonian physics, is the oft-cited twentieth-century example.

3. To distinguish the group of writers and artists best known for their affiliation with *Partisan Review*, I capitalize *Intellectuals*. There were other groups of Jewish intellectuals in New York at other times and composed of different men and women. Irving Howe popularized this designation for the *PR* group in "The New York Intellectuals," *Commentary*, March 1968, 29–51.

4. See John Rodden, ed., *Lionel Trilling and the Critics: Opposing Selves* (Lincoln: University of Nebraska Press, 1999); John Rodden, ed., *The Worlds of Irving Howe* (Boulder, Colo.: Paradigm, 2005); John Rodden, *Irving Howe and the Critics* (Lincoln: University of Nebraska Press, 2005); John Rodden and Ethan Goffman, eds., *Politics and the Intellectual: Conversations with Irving Howe* (West Lafayette, Ind.: Purdue University Press, 2010).

5. The Congress for Cultural Freedom sought to promote the ethos and politics of the West, the so-called Free World, with the goal of convincing European intellectuals to campaign for Western values as the battle against fascism shifted to a battle against communism during the opening decades of the Cold War. The Ransom Center collections are a treasure trove of information about the activities of the group and its branch organizations, such as the New York–based American Committee for Cultural Freedom. Many of the intellectuals affiliated with *Partisan Review* were active both in the Congress for Cultural Freedom and in the American Committee for Cultural Freedom. Nabokov and Josselson conducted correspondence with and about Macdonald in particular as well as with and about many of the other members of the *PR* circle. The Josselson and Nabokov papers are especially valuable because the Congress for Cultural Freedom and its affiliates had been suspected throughout the 1950s and early 1960s of being merely front organizations for the CIA. Rumors swirled for many years that these organizations and their prominent magazines (such as *Encounter* in London and *Der Monat* in Berlin) were funded by the CIA. The New York Intellectuals and other contributors to the magazines hotly denied these rumors, but New Left writers on the staff of *Ramparts* discovered in 1966 that the CIA was indeed both the funding source and the guiding hand behind the Congress and its affiliates. The Josselson papers contain extensive memoranda about this relationship, along with revealing evidence about how both Nabokov and Josselson functioned as CIA agents. On the Congress for Cultural Freedom and the CIA scandal, see Frances Stonor Saunders, *The Cultural Cold War: The CIA and the World of Arts and Letters*

(New York: New Press, 1999). I have also consulted the Michael Josselson Papers and the Nicolas Nabokov Papers at the Ransom Center regarding the activities of the Congress for Cultural Freedom and American Committee for Cultural Freedom during the 1950s and 1960s.

6. The arguments and evidence in these chapters have been revised and fortified with the benefit of the Josselson and Nabokov papers. Where possible, I have also broadened my focus to include selected documents from the State Department and other national security agencies.

7. I have also made selective use of the FBI dossier on Alfred Kazin (1916–97), another elder within the *PR* group and arguably its fourth-leading figure among the seniors. I thank Richard Cook, Kazin's sensitive and erudite biographer, for sharing the dossier with me. Kazin's file begins in 1946 and ends in 1965. In some respects, it resembles those of Trilling and Macdonald. Like Trilling, Kazin attracted the Feds' notice chiefly as a consequence of his connection with other people under investigation—in Kazin's case, Agnes Smedley and I. F. Stone, both of whom were subject to close surveillance because of their communist associations. Like Macdonald, Kazin was the object of a routine check because he knew so many of the invitees to the 1965 White House Festival of the Arts, sponsored by the Johnson administration. The Kazin file totals thirty pages, some of which include blacked-out or redacted areas, which I judged insufficient for a full-length chapter devoted to his case. Moreover, because the issues in his dossier resemble those in the Trilling and Macdonald files, an analysis of the same patterns in the Kazin file would have been superfluous. The Kazin file includes various kinds of information compiled by the FBI because other agencies requested information. For instance, in August 1956 the U.S. Information Agency requested a check on Kazin because it was sponsoring him for foreign travel (under People to People Partners, a literary-cultural outreach program abroad aimed to foster "world understanding" (i.e., to advance American cultural interests in the Third World and to promote the implicit superiority of the "Free World"). Another substantial section of Kazin's dossier pertains to the White House Festival of the Arts, because the Johnson administration ran checks on all artists and intellectuals under consideration for invitations to the White House.

8. For the case supporting intelligence-gathering activities as worthwhile, see the work of Ferdinand Mount, London journalist and head of the Thatcher administration's policy unit in 1982–83. Mount's more programmatic pieces have appeared in his op-ed columns in the *Sunday Times*, *TLS*, and the *Daily Telegraph*. His more substantial essays on national security, intelligence gathering, and policymaking have been collected in his edited volumes, *Communism: A TLS Companion* (Hammersmith: Harvill, 1992); *The British Constitution Now: Recovery or Decline?* (London: Heineman, 1992); *The Recovery of the Constitution* (London: Charter 88 Trust, 1992); and *Private Life 21st Century* (London: Chatto and Windus, 2006).

9. Two authoritative studies that have influenced my thinking and are landmark works of scholarship on the topic are Ellen Schrecker, *Many Are the Crimes: McCarthyism in America* (New York: Little, Brown, 1998); Athan Theoharis, *Chasing Spies:*

How the FBI Failed in Counterintelligence but Promoted the Politics of McCarthyism in the Cold War Years (Chicago: Ivan R. Dee, 2002).

10. Niccolò Machiavelli, *The Prince* (New York: Bantam Classics, 1984).

11. H. S. Ferns, "This Spy Business," *Encounter* 64, No. 5 (May 1985): 57.

12. For a view broadly compatible with my own, see Rhodri Jeffreys-Jones, *Cloak and Dollar: A History of American Secret Intelligence* (New Haven: Yale University Press, 2002), 60–80. See also the work of two other historians based on files released through the Freedom of Information Act: Seth Rosenfeld, *Subversives: The FBI's War on Student Radicals and Reagan's Rise to Power* (New York: Farrar, Straus, and Giroux, 2012); Ivan Greenberg, *The Dangers of Dissent: The FBI and Civil Liberties since 1965* (Lanham, Md.: Lexington Books, 2010).

13. On the Stasi's paralysis amid a wealth of information about its citizenry, see John Rodden, *Dialectics, Dogmas, and Dissent: Stories of East German Victims of Human Rights Abuse* (University Park: Pennsylvania State University Press, 2010); John Rodden, *The Walls That Remain: Western and Eastern Germans since Reunification* (Boulder, Colo.: Paradigm, 2008); John Rodden, *Textbook Reds: Schoolbooks, Ideology, and Eastern German Identity* (University Park: Pennsylvania State University Press, 2006); John Rodden, *Repainting the Little Red Schoolhouse: A History of Eastern German Education, 1945–1995* (New York: Oxford University Press, 2001).

14. See Ferns, "This Spy Business," 57.

15. See Graham Greene, *Our Man in Havana: An Entertainment* (Harmondsworth: Penguin, 1958).

16. See Ferns, "This Spy Business," 57.

17. Ibid. Stimson served as secretary of war in the administrations of Presidents William Howard Taft and Franklin D. Roosevelt and as secretary of state under Herbert Hoover. In 1947, the United States created a modern "intelligence community" to guard against another surprise attack like the one at Pearl Harbor.

Led by a director of central intelligence, the intelligence community consists of thirteen major agencies, among them the FBI (which Theodore Roosevelt informally created in 1908) and the CIA. Seven of the agencies have a predominantly military mission and are within the jurisdiction of the Defense Department (among them, the National Security Agency, which gathers signals intelligence); five are associated with civilian departments, such as the FBI within the Justice Department; and one, the CIA, stands alone as an independent entity that answers directly to the president.

18. For discussion of such matters, see John Rodden, "Heuristics, Hypocrisy, and History without Lessons: Nuremberg, War Crimes, and 'Shock and Awe,'" *Journal of Human Rights* 7, No. 1 (Spring 2008): 34–43. Of course, the government may tighten or loosen regulations and statutes governing release of its material to the public. The George W. Bush administration instituted an extremely restrictive set of criteria, much to the dismay of both scholars and news agencies.

19. See Ferns, "This Spy Business," 57–58. As Ferns notes, "Far more messages are likely to be decrypted due to sloppy cipher and keying procedures by bored operators, defectors, or the retransmission of high-grade material in either low-grade ciphers,

or even plaintext" (59). See also Harry Howe Ransom, "Secret Intelligence in the United States, 1947–1982: The CIA's Search for Legitimacy," in *The Missing Dimension: Government and Intelligence Communities in the Twentieth Century*, ed. Christopher Andrew and David Dilks (Basingstoke: Macmillan, 1984), 199–226.

20. Ferns, "This Spy Business," 61. The FBI is a very different kind of intelligence agency from the CIA. Whereas the CIA both gathers information and promotes de-stabilization, the FBI is a domestic surveillance agency that conducts only the former activity. Other government agencies decide what to do with their information. The FBI sticks to the job of getting reliable information; its extensive networks of informants are not in the business of actively interfering with or undermining the lives of American citizens—unlike, say, the case with the East German Stasi. Nonetheless, the Bureau has periodically engaged in disruptive activities, especially during the Cold War era; for example, the FBI was behind the 1942 Hollywood blacklist and the firing of numerous university professors during the 1940s and 1950s.

21. For an overview of these issues, see Athan Theoharis, *The FBI and American Democracy: A Brief Critical History* (Lawrence: University Press of Kansas, 2004).

22. See Ferns, "This Spy Business," 57–58.

23. This is the image of Trilling in Morris Dickstein's "Foreword: A Man Nobody Ever Knew: Lionel Trilling Remembered," in *Lionel Trilling and the Critics: Opposing Selves*, ed. John Rodden (Lincoln: University of Nebraska Press, 1999), xi–xxiii.

24. George Orwell, "Politics and the English Language," in *The Collected Essays, Journalism, and Letters of George Orwell*, ed. Sonia Orwell and Ian Angos (New York: Harcourt Brace Jovanovich, 1968), 4:128.

25. Dwight Macdonald, "A Critical American," *Twentieth Century*, December 1958. The definitive biography of Macdonald is Michael Wreszin, *A Rebel in Defense of Tradition: The Life and Politics of Dwight Macdonald* (New York: Basic Books, 1995). See also the collection of Macdonald's letters edited by Michael Wreszin, *A Moral Temper* (Chicago: Ivan R. Dee, 2001).

26. See Dwight Macdonald, *Against the American Grain* (New York: Random House, 1962). Fast-forward from Macdonald's case to the present. If FBI agents have traditionally lacked the competence to comprehend the parties and issues on the American Left, imagine how much trouble—linguistically and culturally as well as politically—they doubtless face in the twenty-first century when it comes to investigating alleged post-9/11 threats posed by diverse Arab and Muslim groups.

27. Howe's statement of purpose in *Dissent*'s January 1954 opening issue was titled "Does it Hurt When You Laugh?" It stressed the condition of civil liberties in America.

28. Indeed, Howe's marriage records, his birth certificate, and his military records were all recorded. One report states, "Information was circulated among the Albany bureau for the marriage records of the state of New York, June 15, 1941, and April 12, 1947. The Newark bureau [was contacted] for marriage records and for activities in Princeton, including divorce records, and the New York and Boston bureaus" were also involved.

29. The first Stevenson joke, of course, is an allusion to the famous line in Marx

and Engels's *Communist Manifesto*. The second joke rephrases Lenin's notorious remark about the need for tough disciplinary measures and hardline realpolitik toward "counterrevolutionary" troublemakers, especially intellectuals: "You can't make an omelet without breaking eggs." Cited in Robert North Roberts, Scott John Hammond, and Valerie A. Sulfaro, *Presidential Campaigns, Slogans, Issues, and Platforms: The Complete Encyclopedia* (Santa Barbara, Calif.: Greenwood, 2012), 506.

Conversely, the slipups and shenanigans are not necessarily a license for intellectuals to see themselves as victims of persecution (as Howe acknowledged in his own case). Or as Christopher Hitchens remarks—as if to trump Stevenson as a waggish punster—in "The Egghead's Egger-On," "Intellectuals never sound more foolish than when posing as the last civilised man" (*London Review of Books*, April 27, 2000, 23). The original title for Orwell's *Nineteen Eighty-Four* was "The Last Man of Europe." Unless one lived in a society that exhibited some of the features of the Big Brother state in an advanced form, Hitchens believed, it was unacceptable to view oneself as a victimized Winston Smith.

30. Irving Howe, *A Margin of Hope* (San Diego: Harcourt Brace Jovanovich, 1982), 223, quoted in Edward Alexander, *Irving Howe: Socialist, Critic, Jew* (Indianapolis: Indiana University Press, 2008), 90.

CHAPTER TWO. AN UNLIKELY SUSPECT: LIONEL TRILLING, STALINIST FELLOW TRAVELER?

1. One memo notes: "The FBI has conducted no independent investigation of the above-captioned individual. However, the files of the FBI disclose that Lionel Trilling was listed as a reference by a Communist Party member who admitted to being a member of the Communist Party from March 1941 to about January 1942" (August 28, 1964). That "Communist Party member" was Oliver Snyder, a Trilling student at Columbia in the 1940s who listed Trilling as a reference in the 1950s. See note 22. The FBI Identification Division checked its fingerprint files on several occasions, but Trilling apparently was never fingerprinted.

2. Mark Krupnick writes in *Lionel Trilling and the Fate of Cultural Criticism* (Evanston, Ill.: Northwestern University Press, 1986), "The NCDPP had been organized by the Communist Party in 1931. . . . As in other Communist Party auxiliary organizations, the idea was to use well-known figures like Theodore Dreiser, Lincoln Steffens, and John Dos Passos to win favorable publicity while obscure younger intellectuals like Trilling and his wife carried out the day-to-day administrative chores" (39).

3. The complete file was declassified and released on May 21, 2001.

4. Chambers entered the Communist Party in 1925, joining the staff of the Communist newspaper *Daily Worker* and then the monthly *New Masses*. On Party orders Chambers went underground in 1932 as a Soviet agent, but his increasing dismay with Stalin's show trials and Party purges led him to leave the Party by 1938–39. He soon underwent a full-scale conversion and became a devout Christian and fierce anti-Communist; he began working at *Time* in 1939 and shortly thereafter became

the magazine's foreign editor. On the increasing antagonism felt by liberal American intellectuals toward the USSR and communism after the 1939 Nazi-Soviet pact, see Doug Rossinow, *Visions of Progress: The Left-Liberal Tradition in America* (Philadelphia: University of Pennsylvania Press, 2008). For a liberal anti-communist critique of the American Communist Party specifically during the previous decade, see Judy Kutulas, *The Long War: The Intellectual People's Front and Anti-Stalinism, 1930–1940* (Durham, NC: Duke University Press, 1995).

5. Diana Trilling, *The Beginning of the Journey: The Marriage of Diana and Lionel Trilling* (New York: Mariner, 1993), 216–17. In April 1933, Chambers asked both Diana and Lionel to serve as letter drops for a Soviet espionage project.

6. In the introduction to the 1975 edition of *The Middle of the Journey* (1947; New York: Scribner's, 1975), Trilling says, "We were a group who, for a short time in 1932 and even into 1933, had been in a tenuous relation with the Communist Party through some of its so-called fringe activities" (xvi). Actually, Lionel and Diana Trilling formally converted to communism in the summer of 1931. They were at Yaddo, a writers' retreat in upstate New York. They were converted by Sidney Hook, who was then already an intellectual of note (and Jewish professor in the philosophy department of New York University).

7. Krupnick, *Lionel Trilling*, 41–42. Krupnick notes, "Trilling's break with the Communists in 1933 didn't become public until the next year, when he and twenty-four others, including Edmund Wilson and John Dos Passos, . . . signed an 'Open Letter' to the Party that appeared in its periodical, the *New Masses*" (*Lionel Trilling*, 41).

In addition, according to Krupnick, "As independent radicals, some of the signers withdrew from formal association with any wing of the communist movement. But most in Trilling's circle moved toward one form or another of Trotskyism. They still regarded themselves as communists if not Communists, as an outlawed faction which carried on the ideals of the October Revolution, which the ruling clique in Moscow had betrayed. A few actually joined the Trotskyist organization, the Communist League of America, while others—including Trilling—joined the Non-Partisan Labor Defense, which had been organized in protest against the Stalinist-dominated NCDPP" (Krupnick, *Lionel Trilling*, 42).

8. Stephen Tanner observes in *Lionel Trilling* (Boston: Twayne, 1988), "His political 'activities' in the thirties consisted mainly in writing letters to the editor and signing petitions. For example, in 1934 he and several others wrote a letter to the Communist Party protesting their effort to break up a Socialist rally at Madison Square Garden. Increasingly in the thirties he manifested a detachment from political activism and an inclination to treat literature on the basis of its own adequacy in treating life's complexities rather than for its relevance to class struggle. Trilling admitted that the writings of Marx had a decisive influence on his intellectual life, but it was Marx's method more than his conclusions that interested him" (22). The "Socialist rally" to which Tanner refers is a 1934 anti-Dollfuss rally sponsored by socialists in New York to memorialize their fallen Austrian comrades, which was also the occasion for the joke by Alfred Kazin that I relate at the close of this chapter.

9. Lionel Trilling, *The Journey Abandoned*, edited by Geraldine Murphy (New York: Columbia University Press, 2008); Lionel Trilling, *Matthew Arnold* (New York: Norton, 1939).

10. George Novack (1905–92) joined the communist movement in the United States in 1933 and remained a member and leader of the Socialist Workers Party until his death. As national secretary of the American Committee for the Defense of Leon Trotsky, Novack helped organize the 1937 International Commission of Inquiry (known as the Dewey Commission after its chair, renowned American philosopher John Dewey), which investigated the charges fabricated by Stalin's Moscow trials and met in Mexico City to interview Trotsky. Novack played a prominent role in numerous civil rights battles in subsequent decades, including the landmark lawsuit against FBI spying and disruption won by the Socialist Workers Party in 1986. He was also active in defense of the Cuban Revolution and against the war in Vietnam.

11. The RWL itself had several splits in the 1930s and thereafter. It published a journal, *The Fourth International*. Today it still exists as a section of the International Trotskyist Committee, a small group known for its pro-union activities.

12. This memo was declassified on September 11, 1997, roughly fifty years after the publication of *The Middle of the Journey*.

13. On Andrews's extensive involvement in the Hiss-Chambers case, see Allen Weinstein, *The Hiss-Chambers Case* (New York: Random House, 1994).

14. On August 3, 1948, Chambers, a former Communist Party member, testified under subpoena before the House Committee on Un-American Activities (HUAC) that Hiss had secretly been a Communist while in federal service. Called before HUAC, Hiss categorically denied the charge and was subsequently charged with perjury. A 1949 trial ended in a hung jury, but a second jury found Hiss guilty the following year and sentenced him to five years imprisonment.

Was he guilty? Debate has raged for decades, with left-wing radicals who insist Hiss was framed (as Hiss himself staunchly maintained until his death in 1997) facing off against liberal anti-communists and conservatives who support the conviction and exalt Chambers himself as a culture hero (and his memoir, *Witness*, as a modern spiritual and political classic).

Among the evidence that has emerged in recent years to persuade the majority of American historians of Hiss's guilt are the so-called Venona decryptions, obtained from newly opened Soviet archives after the fall of the USSR in 1991. For a careful study of the declassified Venona documents and their impact on American scholarship, see K. A. Cuordileone, "The Torment of Secrecy: Reckoning with American Communism and Anticommunism after Venona," *Diplomatic History* 35, No. 4 (September 2011): 615–42; Bryan D. Palmer, "Rethinking the Historiography of United States Communism," *American Communist History* 2, No. 2 (2003): 151–70.

15. See Trilling, introduction to *The Middle of the Journey*, , xix. Trilling conceived Gifford Maxim as based on Chambers, "whose commitment to radical politics was meant to be definitive of his whole moral being." Maxim is a "sad comedian," wrote Trilling in his introduction, but in hindsight the Hiss perjury trial showed him to be

a figure of integrity who acted from a "magnanimous intention" (xxxiv). By contrast, fellow-traveling Arthur Croom is loosely based on Hiss.

16. Literary critics have been particularly interested in how Trilling portrayed Chambers in *The Middle of the Journey*, so it is surprising that no FBI agent ever seems to have bothered to read the novel closely (or even venture beyond citing reviews and newspaper summaries). If Hoover's men had done so, they probably would have had a number of insistent questions for Trilling about Chambers's background and Trilling's relationship to Chambers. (The FBI "review" of the book lacks even a single detail about character or plotting.)

17. Every FBI memo and letter refers to Chambers by his full name, Jay David Whittaker Chambers.

18. Some of Chambers's statements referring to Columbia are rather disarming: "To the best of my recollection, I did not do too much of anything during my first two years at Columbia. I was convinced now that my mission in life was to be a Pollack." For Chambers, *Pollack* (or more commonly *Polack*) was a shameful term of denigration, a typical ethnic slur applied to Polish immigrants by middle-class WASPs like himself.

Chambers added during this FBI interview, "I also began writing for the school literary publication, *Morningside*. I remember that I wrote a war story, the exact title of which I have forgotten, but which concerned itself with a fellow who went off to fight the Communists." Chambers recalled that his involvement with the magazine led him to meet a number of other students who were interested in literature and politics, such as Mortimer Adler, who was at the University of Chicago, and Herbert Solow, who became one of the editors of *Fortune* magazine (FBI report, May 11, 1949, 162; two other passages in the report refer to Trilling [230], but both of these references are unexceptional).

19. "Half-forgotten" is probably no exaggeration—and the "revived interest" was both ephemeral and limited to New York cultural circles. Diana Trilling's 1993 memoir notes that Lionel Trilling was chagrined by the reviews of *The Middle of the Journey* and even more by the unwillingness of his publisher, Viking Press, to reprint it when the Hiss-Chambers case dominated the media during 1948–50 and again in 1950–51 after the literary and sales success of *The Liberal Imagination*. After her husband's death, Diana Trilling learned that the editor at Viking, B. W. Huebsch, was a Communist who had privately assisted the Hiss defense. Diana Trilling's memoir shows conclusively that Huebsch blocked a reprint of *The Middle of the Journey* on ideological grounds.

20. Critics of the Smith Act argued that it was an attack on the First Amendment right to free speech, but in June 1951 the U.S. Supreme Court upheld the act by a six-to-two vote. In a dissenting opinion, Justice Hugo Black wrote, "These petitioners were not charged with an attempt to overthrow the government. . . . They were not even charged with saying or writing anything designed to overthrow the government. The charge was that they agreed to assemble and to talk and publish certain ideas at a later date." Black's dissenting opinion did little to slow the federal government's dragnet. Federal prosecutors used it to put on trial native-born politi-

cal radicals suspected of seeking to subvert American institutions and professions. Today, most historians agree that the Smith Act had little to do with a legitimate fear that "revolutionary organizations" were going to overthrow the United States. The purpose was to curtail opposition to the Cold War, whether that opposition came from organized labor, the civil rights movement, or the peace movement. The main victims were left-wing trade unionists.

Other legislative tools used to crush leftist dissent included the Taft-Hartley Act, which required all heads of union locals to take oaths swearing that they were not Communists, and the McCarran Act, which forced members of "revolutionary organizations" to register with the government.

21. New York to Hoover, July 31, 1950, Bufile 100-50311-15, SAC. The Hollywood Ten was a group of screenwriters, directors, and producers who refused to testify before the House Committee on Un-American Activities about their alleged involvement with the Communist Party. Among the other prominent writers denied work beginning in November 1947 because of their supposed political or personal affiliations were Richard Wright, Dashiell Hammett, Dorothy Parker, Lillian Hellman, Langston Hughes, Norman Rosten, Irwin Shaw, Arthur Miller, Louis Untermeyer, and Howard Fast.

22. Typical of these years, the FBI follow-up of a dispatch from the Department of State notes Trilling's support for an Indian anti-communist. On January 20, 2004, the Department of State released a July 22, 1955, dispatch from Bombay in which Trilling expressed support for an action by the Indian Committee for Cultural Freedom (ICCF), which was trying to prevent the deportation of an Indian residing in the United States. This appeal from the ICCF was also supported by the American Committee for Cultural Freedom (ACCF), on which Diana Trilling sat as a board member. Lionel Trilling had signed a letter drafted by James T. Farrell that appeared in *New Leader* (July 11, 1955). Farrell, who was then president of the ACCF, argued that the deportation of this Indian anti-communist would discourage those Asians "who are strongly anti-communist and who may combat the considerable communist influence in the present Indian-Indonesian government." The memo from Bombay to the Department of State had been sent by William T. Turner, the American consul general.

A few years later, in a February 1, 1961, FBI memo, Trilling is cited as having served as an FBI informant for an investigation of Oliver Snyder, Trilling's former student and a member of the Macy's Department Store branch of the CP during 1941–42. Snyder had been an undergraduate at Columbia College between 1946 and 1950 and a graduate student at Columbia University in 1950–51. In July 1960, Snyder submitted a statement to the FBI:

> From about March 1941 to about January 1942, I was a member of the Macy's Department Store branch of the Communist Party. My activities consisted of attending some meetings, classes, parties and rallies. When I went into the U.S. Army I gave up membership and I steadily became more and more disillusioned with the whole movement. After my escape from a German prison camp, I was in Poland and Russia for a month and saw the Russians at first hand. Ever since this time I have been a confirmed and consistent fighter against Communism, as

my references can testify. Attached is an anti-communist article that I published in *Commentary*, a leading anti-communist magazine.

The article was "Report on the American Communist," *Commentary*, February 1953.

23. "On May 21–22, 1961, a confidential informant who has furnished reliably accurate information in the past made available the names and addresses of individuals and organizations maintained . . . by the Fair Play for Cuba Committee." Trilling's name was on this list. Trilling's FBI file dated August 28, 1964, contains the full report on these matters.

24. The FBI memo also referred to a *Chicago Daily Tribune* article pertaining to Russian Jews, noting that the "considerable interest in regard to the treatment of Soviet Jews in Russia"·is developing both "in conservative as well as in progressive Jewish organizations."

25. On September 9, 1960, the FBI processed a request for "subversive references only" pertaining to Trilling's background check. But the file does not explain the reasons for or context of this check.

26. Diana Trilling, "A Visit to Camelot," *New Yorker*, June 2, 1997, 54; Lionel Trilling, *The Liberal Imagination: Essays on Literature and Society* (New York: Viking, 1950).

27. The screening of Trilling was requested by the associate counsel to President Johnson, Lee C. White. A February 1, 1965, memo from the White House to the FBI noted that Trilling is "a leading professor of American literature and is spending this year at Oxford." The White House memorandum also requested a name check of Trilling, apparently to verify whether—like so many other former Trotskyists and CP members—he had adopted a party name. (Or whether, like many members of immigrant Jewish families, he had Americanized his name to facilitate assimilation, since "Trilling" certainly does not sound like a name of a family from Białystok. But that name is indeed Trilling's original family name.)

28. Macdonald went to the White House deliberately dressed down in a plaid shirt and tennis shoes, spent the day trying to collect signatures for his petition denouncing the Johnson administration, and then wrote scathingly about the festival in a piece for the *New York Review of Books*. For the hilarious full story of his experience, including selections from Macdonald's FBI dossier, see John Rodden and John Rossi, "Kultur Clash at the White House: Dwight Macdonald and the 1965 Festival of the Arts," *Kenyon Review* 29, No. 4 (Fall 2007): 161–81.

29. Just as Trilling's file expanded enormously because of his personal connection with Chambers and the fact that Trilling's novel included a character based on Chambers, Kazin's file consists in large part of material that the FBI included because he had joined various communists and leftists in signing open letters addressed to numerous newspapers. For example, Kazin's dossier was created because a March 1946 issue of the *New York Times* publicized a letter signed by Kazin that criticized Chiang Kai-shek for arresting and mistreating a vocal anti-Nationalist who died in prison. Other signatories to the letter included Elizabeth Ames, the director of the Yaddo artist community in upstate New York; and Agnes Smedley, an American

communist sympathizer. The letter claimed that Chiang had imprisoned Yang Chao, a Chinese editor-writer, for six months "without charge or trial" and was therefore "fully responsible" for his death.

One FBI memo in the Kazin file described Smedley as "a non-Russian member of Soviet Intelligence" who was in regular contact with "numerous Communists and Communist sympathizers." In 1949, Smedley was publicly accused of spying for the USSR. When reports circulated that she had traveled with Mao Zedong to report on the Chinese Communist Revolution, she had already been a visiting guest writer at Yaddo from 1943 to 1948. Documents in the former Soviet archives support claims that Smedley did indeed serve as a spy for the Comintern during the Stalin years. It is known that she applied for membership to the Chinese Communist Party but was rejected because she was viewed as too independent. (Partly because of Smedley's close association with Yaddo, Ames was also investigated by the FBI, but she was cleared of all charges.)

Another section of Kazin's file reflects the FBI's interest in a different letter that he cosigned. The Johnson administration received a June 1965 letter supporting Robert Lowell's decision not to participate in the Festival of the Arts the following August. Because Kazin and two dozen other members of the intellectual and artistic community had signed a public letter supporting Lowell, the FBI reopened Kazin's file. Other public statements by Kazin that attracted the FBI's notice included a letter he cosigned in 1964 castigating the activities of the House Un-American Activities Committee (HUAC) and arguing that the committee should cease "investigation into the peace movement."

On Smedley's activities as a foreign correspondent during the Chinese Civil War and foreign agent for the Soviet Union, see Ruth Price, *The Lives of Agnes Smedley* (Oxford: Oxford University Press, 2005).

Since the breakup of the USSR in December 1991, conduct of Soviet espionage in the United States has become a prominent topic in twenty-first-century scholarship devoted to American communism. Among the best literature on the topic of American communism and Soviet espionage are Harvey Klehr, John Earl Haynes, and Fridrikh Igorevich Firsov, *The Secret World of American Communism* (New Haven: Yale University Press, 1995); Harvey Klehr, John Earl Haynes, and Alexander Vassiliev, *Spies: The Rise and Fall of the KGB in America* (New Haven: Yale University Press, 2009). See also R. Bruce Craig, *Treasonable Doubt: The Harry Dexter White Spy Case* (Lawrence: University Press of Kansas, 2004); John Earl Haynes and Harvey Klehr, *In Denial: Historians, Communism and Espionage* (San Francisco: Encounter, 2003).

30. All this is not to suggest that the FBI would have found Trilling's literary criticism or even political-intellectual journalism directly relevant to its investigations. Rather, even minimal acquaintance with that work would have given FBI agents a sense of the preoccupations of the intellectuals whom they were investigating—and perhaps helped Hoover's men to avoid some of the misunderstandings or misconceptions that they developed about the Trotskyist "eggheads" during the Cold War.

31. Philip Roth, *The Prague Orgy* (New York: Farrar, Straus, and Giroux, 1985), 65.

32. Kazin later published a version of the story. See Alfred Kazin, "Rewriting the Thirties," *Intellectual History Newsletter* 19 (1997): 50.

33. And in yet another irony, the blundering incapacity of the G-men to grasp the complexities of American left-wing sectarian groups represented a striking counterface image resembling the confusions within the American Left itself. Many American ex-Communists argued that communism had emerged as a dialectical outgrowth of liberalism's utopian emphasis on individual freedom, making liberals and liberalism alike ultimately culpable for the crimes of communism. In this view, liberals were not just guilty but utterly incapable of understanding and combating communism. Ex-Communists alone understood communism and how to fight it. As Ignazio Silone once famously phrased it, the final battle would necessarily be between the Communists and the ex-Communists. Under such conditions, the "old" oppositions—socialism versus capitalism, Left versus Right—were passé. The realities of Stalinist tyranny dictated that the only relevant choice was that of "freedom" versus "slavery"—or, rather, bourgeois democracy, with all its shortcomings, versus collectivist tyranny. Like many ex-Communists, James Burnham believed that because former Communists alone could comprehend what "the final battle" was all about, they should constitute the party or avant-garde that would lead the charge against international communism.

34. Lionel Trilling, "Our Country and Our Culture: A Symposium," *Partisan Review* 19, No. 3 (1952): 318–26.

35. Irving Howe and Nina Howe, *A Voice Still Heard: Selected Essays of Irving Howe* (New Haven: Yale University Press, 2014), 3–25; Delmore Schwartz, "The Duchess' Red Shoes," *Partisan Review* 20, No. 1 (1953): 55–73; Joseph Frank, "Lionel Trilling and the Conservative Imagination," *Salmagundi* 41 (1978): 33–54.

36. The interest of American intellectuals and historians in the connections between Trilling and Chambers, however, has not been as arbitrary or accidental. With justice, both Trilling and Chambers have been paired as decisive influences contributing significantly to "the conservative turn" of the 1950s, with Chambers exerting influence from the right and Trilling from the left. Although the two men rarely met after their student days in the early 1920s, their lives and legacies warrant comparison and reflection, given the roles of religion in their outlooks and their similar, if quite distinctive, verdicts on the fate of Western civilization. Indeed, their careers raise large questions both about the course of American intellectual history and about politics and culture in the twentieth century, for they were important actors in and witnesses to some of its major developments.

For a different point of view on these and other topics related to Trilling and Chambers, see Michael Kimmage, "Trilling the Communist" (unpublished essay, 2005). This essay was later modified for a section of Kimmage's *The Conservative Turn: Lionel Trilling, Whittaker Chambers, and the Lessons of Anti-Communism* (Cambridge: Harvard University Press, 2009), 15–45. Others have disputed the contention that Trilling made "a conservative turn." Diana Trilling, for one, insisted that Trilling never would have become a neoconservative and that he never moved to the right.

37. This fact raises another irony that Trilling would have appreciated. Representing a narrative in sepia of his shadowy past—starkly contrasting with his public persona at midcentury as one of America's first academic celebrities—Trilling's FBI file inadvertently mirrors Trilling's approach to his own and his friends' Stalinism in *The Middle of the Journey*. The novel thematizes how the past shadows us—that is, how the pastness in the present haunts the lives of all its major characters.

Indeed, although most of the novel's characters have had relations of varying intimacy to the CP in the past, those relations have long ended. Yet as the novel demonstrates, they have not so much ceased as been transformed, for the past lives on in the present in unexpected ways—that is, in the forms of personal loyalties (or claims on such loyalties), in antagonisms rooted in old ideological divisions (or more recently diverging pasts), and in the urgent need for renewal and replenishment after years of personal sacrifice and disillusionment.

38. Kimmage, "Trilling the Communist." The topic is also discussed in Kimmage, *Conservative Turn*, especially chapter 2, p. 58.

39. This is not to imply that Trilling overlooked or rationalized away the economic and political injustices of American society, especially during his temporary radical phase in the 1930s. Even after his brief fellow-traveling year as a member of a Communist-front organization had long passed, he never closed an eye to racial and class inequalities, though his liberal stance increasingly stressed America's progress toward easing such disparities (unlike Macdonald and particularly Howe, both of whom delivered sharper post-war critiques of American society).

A further reminder of Trilling's critical albeit reflective and searching attitude toward Western capitalism generally and American bourgeois life in particular comes with the recent appearance of his never-completed novel, *The Journey Abandoned*. This bildungsroman features Vincent Hammell, a cross between Trilling himself and selected aspects of both Kazin and Howe. Hammell is an ambitious young critic-historian, keenly interested in the relations among literature, morality, and society (like Trilling) and diligently at work on a history of nineteenth-century American literature (like Kazin, who at twenty-six published *On Native Grounds* [1942], a precocious study of American fiction from 1870 to the 1930s). The Howe connection is even more likely. In the preface to *The Journey Abandoned*, Murphy cites a Trilling journal entry from 1948 pondering Howe's rising prominence as an intellectual and critic. Trilling exclaims, "How right for my Vincent!" Moreover, by 1952 Trilling is mulling whether he might rekindle his commitment to the novel by making Vincent "specifically Jewish," a description he was more apt to use for Howe than for Kazin.

Set in the Great Depression, the novel thematizes success versus failure as it poses Vincent's dilemmas between perceived corruption and moral heroism. Trilling completed only one-third of the novel before abandoning it (and his attempts to write fiction); the work totals 153 pages in twenty-four chapters.

40. A former student of Trilling from the early 1950s—the apex of Trilling's critical and public reputation—essentially agrees with me on this point after reading this chapter. He is a vocal advocate of strong American security forces, including the

intelligence services. Nonetheless, quite irate, he also writes, "It is amazing that these FBI dopes read almost nothing of what LT had written, including his mockeries of ideologies like Marxism in *The Middle of the Journey* and his short stories. But they were good at following him and Diana to Grand Central Station (or was it Penn Station?)! They read *Middle of the Journey* because of the Chambers connection, but didn't register the meaning of the *Daily Worker* reacting to it with hysterical hostility. The idea that the FBI dossier on LT nevertheless traces the shadow life of LT's numerous personal connections with Communists is intriguing" (Edward Alexander, personal communication, April 2015).

41. Trilling certainly was never followed as closely as such other literary targets of FBI (and even CIA) probes as Ernest Hemingway, Pearl S. Buck, Sinclair Lewis, John Steinbeck, William Faulkner, W. H. Auden, Truman Capote, John Dos Passos, Tennessee Williams, Thomas Wolfe, and Thornton Wilder. On their scrutiny by U.S. intelligence agencies, see Herbert Mitgang, *Dangerous Dossiers: Exposing the Secret War against America's Greatest Authors* (New York: Fine, 1988); Angus Mackenzie, *Secrets: The CIA's War at Home* (Berkeley: University of California Press, 1997).

42. On the Congress for Cultural Freedom and the CIA scandal, see Frances Stonor Saunders, *The Cultural Cold War: The CIA and the World of Arts and Letters* (London: New Press, 1999).

CHAPTER THREE. FROM FBI NOSE-TWEAKER TO CIA "STOOGE" TO LBJ'S NEMESIS: DWIGHT MACDONALD, A "CRITICAL (UN?)AMERICAN"

1. Hoover was appointed director of the Bureau of Investigation (predecessor to the FBI) in 1924. When the FBI was founded in 1935, he became its director until his death in 1972.

2. The definitive biography of Macdonald is Michael Wreszin, *A Rebel in Defense of Tradition: The Life and Politics of Dwight Macdonald* (New York: Basic Books, 1994). See also the collection of Macdonald's letters edited by Wreszin, *A Moral Temper* (Chicago: Dee, 2001).

3. Cited in Herbert Mitgang, *Dangerous Dossiers: Exposing the Secret War against America's Greatest Authors* (New York: Fine, 1988), 29.

4. See John Rodden, *Irving Howe and the Critics* (Lincoln: University of Nebraska Press, 2004); John Rodden, ed., *The Worlds of Irving Howe* (Boulder, Colo.: Paradigm, 2005).

5. Oscar Wilde, *The Writings of Oscar Wilde* (London: Keller, 1907), 16.

6. Quoted in Gregory D. Sumner, *Dwight Macdonald and the Politics Circle: The Challenge of Cosmopolitan Democracy* (Ithaca: Cornell University Press, 1996), 6.

7. Quoted in Sumner, *Dwight Macdonald and the Politics Circle*, 6.

8. See Ellen Schrecker, *Many Are the Crimes: McCarthyism in America* (New York: Little, Brown, 1998); Athan Theoharis, *Chasing Spies: How the FBI Failed in Counter-*

intelligence but Promoted the Politics of McCarthyism in the Cold War Years (Chicago: Dee, 2002).

9. Report on Dwight Macdonald, April 6, 1944, Bufile 100-268519-8.

10. Ibid.

11. Ibid.

12. On Zanuck's disinclination to enter into a deal with Hoover for a series of pro-FBI films, see Clyde Tolson to Hoover, April 22, 1947, Bufile 44-4-38-323-2.

13. New York to Hoover, September 3, 1947, Bufile 100-268519-SAG.

14. Ibid.

15. Tolson to Hoover, April 23, 1947, Bufile 100-268519-G. Attached to this memorandum is a notation in Hoover's handwriting, "Let us make a discreet investigation of this outfit."

16. New York to Hoover, September 3, 1947, Bufile 100-268519-SAG.

17. Hoover, memo, n.d. [ca. autumn–winter 1947–48].

18. Clifton Bennett, "The F.B.I.," *politics*, Winter 1948, 19–26.

19. New York to Hoover, December 20, 1957, Bufile 100-268519-70, SAC.

20. New York to Hoover, April 4, 1958, Bufile 100-268519-74.

21. A. H. Belmont to L. V. Boardman, April 6, 1958, Bufile 100-268519-75. Macdonald's report on the Waldorf Conference can be found in the April 1949 *politics*. It was reprinted in the London journal *Horizon* the following month. For an overview of the Waldorf Conference, see John P. Rossi, "Farewell to Fellow-Traveling: The Waldorf Peace Conference of 1949," *Continuity: A Journal of History* 10 (Spring 1983): 1–31.

22. Memorandum for Hoover, January 31, 1961, Bufile 100-268519.

23. See the correspondence for 1957–58 between Josselson and Macdonald in the Michael Josselson Papers, box 22, folder 7, Harry Ransom Center, University of Texas at Austin.

24. See Dwight Macdonald, "A Critical American," *Twentieth Century*, December 1958. Indignant toward the British editors for their intervention, Macdonald penned his letter proudly. He had already sent the essay to his former assistant at *politics*, Irving Howe. He added his own introduction, which included his version of events regarding his shabby treatment by his colleagues at *Encounter*. On these matters, see Wreszin, *Rebel*, 537.

25. Josselson to Hunt, May 27, 1958, Josselson Papers, box 22, folder 7. See also Dwight Macdonald, "America, America," *Dissent*, Autumn 1958, 313–23.

26. Josselson to Kristol, October 30, 1958, Josselson Papers, box 22, folder 7.

27. Josselson to Macdonald, March 15, 1967, in ibid., box 26, folder 4.

28. See Wreszin, *Rebel*. See also Macdonald, *Moral Temper*.

29. Indeed Macdonald's breast-beating sometimes possesses a shrillness that leaves the impression that "he doth protest too much." Spender's professions of innocence (or rather "invincible ignorance," as unsympathetic colleagues chortled) frequently sounded a similar note. Could two such intelligent, widely traveled, sociable men with many skeptical radical friends have had no inkling of the truth? Could they have been so gullible as to have dismissed all the rumors that were in the air for

years? Were they utterly blind to Cold War realpolitik? Were they so obtuse that after many years as contributors to (and, in Spender's case, as the British editor of) *Encounter*, they really did not know until after the scandal broke that some American intelligence agency was connected to the magazine and the CCF, probably in some kind of money-laundering scheme? Were they so naive as to think that the lavish international conferences, expensive airfares, and sumptuous meals all came from a good-hearted, disinterested cultural benefactor (Julius Fleisher)? It all seems unlikely.

By the same token, as worldly figures such as Malcolm Muggeridge and Fred Warburg remarked at the time: Was the "scandal" such a big deal? Or instead a tempest in a teapot? As a friend of mine began an essay that treated a related clandestine project, "I used to work for the CIA." By that he meant simply that he had inadvertently been employed by a cultural front group that the CIA had funded. "Who knew? Well, not me," he said. Like Warburg and Muggeridge, he was not particularly upset by the news, let alone humiliated. He was a young man and a mere intern in a CIA cultural project. He didn't ask any questions, and no one delivered bombshell revelations to him before the news of the scandal. Macdonald, like Spender, was not in this position, and both his heated denials and strenuous remonstrations often seem strained.

On the personal relations between CCF officials headquartered in Paris (Josselson, Nicolas Nabokov, John C. Hunt) and the British Committee of the CCF in London (which was headed by Muggeridge and Warburg), see the Josselson Papers, especially boxes 22–26. See also the Nicolas Nabokov Papers, Ransom Center. Nabokov was the secretary-general of the international CCF. He published his autobiography with Warburg's house, Secker and Warburg. Hunt was a CCF staff member who became the CCF's executive secretary in Paris in the 1970s, soon after Macdonald published "America! America!" and returned to the United States.

30. Cited in Wreszin, *Rebel*, 88, 452.

31. William Barrett, *The Truants: Adventures among the Intellectuals* (New York: Anchor/Doubleday, 1982), 221.

32. A. Jones to G. DeLoach, November 5, 1962, Bufile 100-268519-80.

33. Wreszin, *Rebel*, 482.

34. For a full discussion of Macdonald's actions at the White House Conference on the Arts, see John Rodden and John Rossi, "Kultur Clash at the White House: Dwight Macdonald and the 1965 Festival of the Arts," *Kenyon Review* 29, No. 4 (Fall 2007): 161–81.

35. Dwight Macdonald, "A Day at the White House," *New York Review of Books*, July 15, 1965, in Macdonald, *Discriminations: Essays and Afterthoughts, 1938–1974* (New York: Viking, 1974), 140–54.

36. Eric F. Goldman, *The Tragedy of Lyndon Johnson* (New York: Knopf, 1969), 450.

37. According to an FBI memo, Gingrich added that Macdonald "has always been concerned with morality in whatever area he has chosen to write on over the years and he considers him to be one of the outstanding moralists of the time. He described him as an individual of superb character. He stated that several great literary figures of

the world considered the appointee to be the most brilliant essayist in the English language today. He added that Macdonald is forever seeking justice, truth and equality."

38. For example, a January 28, 1965, memo notes that Macdonald is "well-known to Richard Roviere" (a misspelling of *Rovere*) and is "also well-known to Arthur Schlesinger, Jr." The memo included enclosures such as Schlesinger's review of Macdonald's *Henry Wallace: The Man and the Myth* (New York: Vanguard, 1948), William Barrett's review of Macdonald's *Memoirs of a Revolutionist* (New York: Farrar, Straus, and Cudahy, 1957), and Leslie Fiedler's review of Macdonald's *Against the American Grain* (New York: Random House, 1962). The reviews by Schlesinger, Barrett, and Fiedler all appeared in the *New York Times Book Review*. The titles suggest the flavors of both the reviews and Macdonald's books: see Arthur Schlesinger Jr., "The Apostle of the Common Man: A Portrait Etched in Acid," *New York Times Book Review*, February 22, 1948, 3; William Barrett, "Spokesman for Himself," *New York Times Book Review*, September 22, 1957, 304; Leslie Fiedler, "A Voice in Opposition," *New York Times Book Review*, April 21, 1963, 12.

39. Macdonald's voting records disclosed that he had indicated a preference for the Communist Party in 1933, 1934, and 1936 and for the American Labor Party in 1937, 1940, and 1941. Macdonald had been in London between June 1, 1956, and September 7, 1957, in Spain from April to August 1935, and in France and England from April to June 1933.

40. The FBI also obtained the July 1, 1964, divorce records from the registrar's office in Montgomery, Alabama.

41. A February 1, 1965, memo concludes that "associates and neighbors recommend Macdonald as a loyal American of good character." Macdonald himself would certainly have scoffed at that description. As we have seen, since he had told the editors of *Twentieth Century* in 1958 that he was not "A Good American" but rather "A Critical American." Another interviewee described Macdonald "as a highly confident writer who is very argumentative and extreme at times in his statements; on the other hand, Macdonald is very good-natured. Appointee can also be described as an intellectual who is 'very vocal.'"

42. Goldman, *Tragedy*, 446. At the opening of the festival, LBJ put in a perfunctory appearance, read a meaningless statement, and then absented himself from the rest of the proceedings.

43. Goldman, *Tragedy*, 419.

44. Wreszin, *Rebel*, 403.

45. Macdonald, *Moral Temper*, 368–69.

46. Wreszin, *Rebel*, 402.

47. The organizer was B. Diamondstein, quoted in Emilie Raymond, *From My Cold, Dead Hands: Charlton Heston and American Politics* (Lexington: University Press of Kentucky, 2006), 136.

48. Heston was most outraged by Macdonald's discourtesy to his hosts: "Are you really accustomed to signing petitions against your host in his home?" Heston allegedly shouted. Jack Valenti, a special assistant to the president who soon became

head of the Motion Picture Association of America, later recalled with "undying pleasure" how Heston "just ate [Macdonald's] ass out" for his ignorance of "propriety" and "then he gave Macdonald precise directions to what he can do with his petitions, and they were very precise" (quoted in Raymond, *From My Cold, Dead Hands*, 136).

49. Wreszin, *Rebel*, 400. With the exception of the painter Willem de Kooning, the signatories were not a high-profile lot: the sculptor Herbert Ferber, the artist-sculptor Isamu Noguchi, and biographer Reed Whittemore were the only recognizable names among them. But Macdonald insisted that "it was significant that nobody refused to sign because he favored the president's foreign policy."

50. Ibid.

51. Goldman, *Tragedy of Lyndon Johnson*, 475.

52. Macdonald, "Day at the White House," in *Discriminations*, 154.

53. Generally speaking, this state of affairs has even prevailed during the Obama administration, notwithstanding the fact that Barack Obama is the most intellectual president since fellow former professor Woodrow Wilson occupied the White House a century earlier. Certainly no president received more kudos from (liberal) intellectuals since the Kennedy years than did Obama, though the applause has dwindled during his second term to near silence, especially on the liberal left—and been replaced by a rising chorus of criticism.

54. Macdonald, *Moral Temper*, 368–69.

55. Ibid., 374–75.

56. Wreszin, *Rebel*, 415.

57. Ibid., 477.

58. Macdonald, *Moral Temper*, 157.

59. Ibid., 165.

60. Ibid., 179.

61. Special Agent in Charge, New York, to Hoover, April 30, 1970, Bufile 100-268519-92.

62. One hopeful note, however, is that Macdonald's two outstanding long essays devoted to anarchism that originally appeared in *politics*, "The Root Is Man" and "The Responsibility of Peoples," have been reprinted by Auto-Media, a publisher that specializes in libertarian books. Even more welcome is the news that the republication of a selection of his best essays has generated a slight resurgence of interest in him.

An almost universal silence had prevailed in 2006 on the centennial of his birth— unlike the case of Trilling, whose centennial was commemorated widely in the United States via academic conferences and numerous memorials—and on the twenty-fifth anniversary of his death in December 2007. This turn of events is welcome news. By contrast, the publication of *Masscult and Midcult: Essays against the American Grain*, edited by John Summers (New York: New York Review Books, 2011), received a good bit of fanfare. Substantial, laudatory review essays of Macdonald's career have appeared in the leading journals of opinion and magazines on the left and the liberal left. Time will tell whether this development is only temporary. See, for example, Louis Menand, "Browbeaten: Dwight Macdonald's War on Midcult," *New Yorker*, September 5, 2011, 72–78; Dwight Garner, "Dwight Macdonald's War on Mediocrity," *New York Times Book Review*, October 21, 2011, 35; Jennifer Szalai, "Mac the Knife: On Dwight Macdonald," *Nation*, November 21, 2011, 18–23; Franklin Foer, "The Browbeater," *New Republic*, November 23, 2011, 27–32; Scott McLemee, "Intellectual Affairs," *Inside Higher Ed*, November 30, 2011; Clive James, "Style Is the Man," *The Atlantic*, May 2012, 92–98.

63. George Orwell, "Freedom of the Press," *Times Literary Supplement*, September 15, 1972. Macdonald was the lone New York Intellectual to develop a relationship with Orwell, conducting a vigorous correspondence with him from 1942 until Orwell's death in 1950. They agreed broadly on both political and cultural matters. But Macdonald was much more insistent on upholding "classical" standards and cultural norms. For example, whereas Orwell held that those who "really cared for the art of the novel" were "neither highbrows nor lowbrows nor midbrows, but elastic-brows" (George Orwell, "In Defence of the Novel," in *George Orwell: The Collected Essays, Journalism, and Letters*, ed. Sonia Orwell and Ian Angus [Boston: Godine, 2000], 1:254), Macdonald remained (by his own admission) an unreconstructed curmudgeon and literary snob, adamantly equating artistic excellence (indeed, artistic integrity) with highbrow taste and traditional "elitist" standards.

64. See Macdonald, *Against the American Grain*, 156.

CHAPTER FOUR. WANTED BY THE FBI?
IRVING HORENSTEIN, #7384A AKA
"REVOLUTIONARY CONSPIRATOR" IRVING HOWE

1. The sectarian squabbles of the 1940s within the Trotskyist movement, which led to the formation of the ISL, were complex. A faction led by Max Shachtman split off from the Socialist Workers Party (SWP) in 1940 to create the Worker's Party (WP). They were the minority and claimed they were expelled; the majority, led by James Cannon, claimed that Shachtman had initiated the split. All this occurred in the wake of the Hitler-Stalin Pact of 1939, which caused a crisis in the SWP days after the Soviet Union attacked Poland and the Baltic States. Some intellectuals associated with Shachtman, such as James Burnham, announced that the USSR was a new form of class society, but Shachtman's view of "the Russian Question" was still in formation.

The rupture came to a head over organizational issues, and in subsequent months (after the split) Shachtman's new view of the USSR evolved: at first the USSR was superior to the Western imperialist countries, then both were equally bad, and finally Shachtman advocated critical support for the West. The name switch from WP to ISL mainly came from the WP's recognition that it couldn't regard itself as a party when it was basically a political agitprop group. (Shachtman loyalists in the SWP followed him and joined the ISL, whose members became known as the Shachtmanites and whose membership in 1943 was approximately five hundred.)

2. Several FBI regional bureaus received copies of Howe's birth records, marriage records, army records from the Boston office of the Department of Veterans Affairs, fingerprinting and other army records, and even photographs from the City College of New York.

3. One FBI entry begins: "Irving Horenstein was the true name of one Irving Howe." The file repeatedly notes that "Horenstein is his true surname" and refers to the subject's "alias" as "Irving Howe." It observes that "the middle name Arthur is added as shown in the birth records of the subject's children."

4. The American embassy wrote on November 19, 1957, to the director of the FBI that the Paris police had discovered a suitcase containing male and female clothing and that the owner of the suitcase was Howe. (Howe had lectured at the Salzburg Seminar in Austria that summer.) It is interesting that the American embassy chose to contact the FBI to get in touch with Howe.

5. Edward Alexander, *Irving Howe: Socialist, Critic, Jew* (Bloomington: Indiana University Press, 1998), 94.

6. See ibid., chapter 5, "The Fifties: Age of Conformity, Age of Dissent."

7. The FBI file on Alfred Kazin also includes memoranda about his activities criticizing the House Un-American Activities Committee a decade later. For example, Kazin supported various calls in the early 1960s to abolish the committee. In December 1962, the *Daily Worker* mentioned Kazin as one of fifty Americans who had demanded that the committee cancel its proposed investigation of the "peace movement." Marvin Watson, special assistant to President Lyndon Johnson, had requested the FBI files of the two dozen signatories to the telegram in support of Robert Lowell's refusal to attend the 1965 White House Festival of the Arts.

Kazin largely shared Howe's political outlook but never participated in any socialist (let alone Trotskyist) agitation except for signing a few letters in support of various left-wing causes. So although Kazin's political positions were not far removed from those of Howe, Kazin saw himself first as a self-reliant Emersonian individualist and a literary-cultural critic and only secondarily as a political being. Kazin adopted a broadly socialist or Left stance yet lacked the formal organizational commitments or activist style of Howe. As Richard Cook states in his excellent biography of Kazin, "Though he and Howe shared roughly the same political views, often found themselves on the same panels, and eventually became colleagues in the English Department at the City University of New York, Kazin would continue to see him as an unreconstructed 'ideologue,' ready for the next political fight—the hardened, eager veteran of the City College alcove wars." (*Alfred Kazin: A Biography* [New Haven: Yale University Press, 2008], 130). Kazin's FBI file was declassified in December 2005.

8. On Howe's conflicts with leaders of Students for a Democratic Society such as Tom Hayden and Todd Gitlin, see John Rodden, ed., *The Worlds of Irving Howe* (Boulder, Colo.: Paradigm, 2005), 164–65; Todd Gitlin, "Looking Back on the New Left and the Counterculture," in *Politics and the Intellectual: Conversations with Irving*

Howe, ed. John Rodden and Ethan Goffman (West Lafayette, Ind.: Purdue University Press, 2010), 151–98.

9. See, for example, John Rodden, "The Galileo of the GDR: Robert Havemann," *Debatte* 14, No. 1 (April 2006): 37–48. Havemann (1910–82) was an East German dissident scientist who was banned from publishing any of his work beginning in the early 1960s and was subjected to permanent house arrest from 1976 until his death. A revised version of this article appears in John Rodden, *Dialectics, Dogmas, and Dissent* (University Park: Pennsylvania State University Press, 2010).

10. A 1955 file notes, "New York office reports on May 11, 1955, [based] on records of the Bureau of Vital Statistics from the Bronx: Irving Howe's marriage at the age of 20, his parents both listed as having been born in Russia."

11. The timing of the opening of Howe's FBI file may have been triggered by his controversial and widely reported public dispute with Sidney Hook over the disciplinary action taken against six professors at the University of Washington in Seattle, all of whom were either current or former members of the American Communist Party. Three of them were fired outright and three others suspended. Hook supported the university's decision, whereas Howe defended the right of the professors to keep their jobs even though he disagreed fiercely with their Stalinist allegiances. Howe's defense of the professors' civil rights despite their CP membership would likely have raised eyebrows with the security agencies.

12. Alexander, *Irving Howe*, 19.

13. Howe indeed had two children, but one was a girl. See Boston FBI report, September 15, 1954, for the error. Another report notes, "Birth records were also searched in New York for the subject's two male children. The New York bureau checked under the name Horenstein for the boys' names." An Albany bureau report (March 31, 1955) noted that "a check of birth records, from 1941 to date, under the name Horenstein reflected only one male born during that period with this name. A check of this record reflected that this was not one of the subject's children." (Howe's children are Nicholas and Nina.)

14. For several years, Howe had been wavering about his ISL affiliation. He was writing less and less for Trotskyist publications and turning his attention from Trotskyist to literary matters, having just completed a study of Sherwood Anderson (1951) and begun one on William Faulkner (1952). He had begun contributing articles and reviews to *Partisan Review* in the late 1940s. Perhaps his decision to resign from the ISL in October 1952 was accelerated by his first college teaching experience the preceding summer at the University of Washington in Seattle. In a department dominated by leftists despite the firing of three professors who were members of the Communist Party in 1949, Howe found himself drawn toward the conservative New Critics in the English Department, with the single exception of his cordial relationship with anarchist Wayne Burns, with whom Howe shared an admiration for writers such as Orwell. For Howe's reflections on this period of his life, see Robert B. Heilman,

Robert B. Heilman: His Life in Letters, edited by Edward Alexander, Richard Dunn, and Paul Jaussen (Seattle: University of Washington Press, 2009), 704.

15. The Draper-Howe exchange is discussed in Alexander, *Irving Howe*, 95–96. Howe was already at odds with the ISL because of its failure to support the Marshall Plan and to align itself unequivocally with the Western powers against the spread of communism. In 1951, Howe and Plastrik tried to persuade the ISL, which sponsored *Labor Action*, to sponsor also a quarterly journal that would be similar in style and substance to the defunct *politics*. The ISL refused. See Gerald Sorin, *Irving Howe: A Life of Passionate Dissent* (New York: New York University Press, 2002).

16. Alexander, *Irving Howe*, 74.

17. This was the case at the time of the final release date of Howe's full file to me in 1997.

18. See Alexander, *Irving Howe*, chapter 5, "The Fifties: Age of Conformity, Age of Dissent." The comment is quoted from Abram Leon Sachar, *Brandeis University: A Host at Last* (rev. ed., Hanover, N.H.: University Press of New England for Brandeis University Press, 1995), 143.

19. Several FBI memos repeated the caution voiced by one Bureau official: "This investigation must be conducted in accordance with the provisions set forth in the manual of instructions relating to security-type investigations at institutions of learning." Another Boston memo added, "Interview with Irving Horenstein ok'd, so long as it must be conducted in a particularly circumspect manner, so that no embarrassment to the Bureau will result."

20. The three lectures were delivered to the University of Chicago Politics Club (October 14, 1949, on "The Need For a Worker's Party"), to the Socialist Youth League (August 13, 1949, on "Bureaucracy in Trade Unions"), and to the ISL (September 23, 1949, on "Bureaucracy and Democracy in the Labor Movement"). The Politics Club was a Trotskyist group that had been reactivated by the Chicago branch of the Young People's Socialist League in the fall of 1947.

21. Another FBI memo hilariously refers to "Suitable telephonic pretext, Brandeis University," a good example of the jargon that the FBI used to make a phone call check.

22. This information appears in the March 31, 1959, dossier compiled by the Boston office, which also includes the editorial statement of purpose from the opening issue of *Dissent*.

23. *Dissent* launched its first forum in November 1954 in New York City. By 1958, a half dozen *Dissent* groups in various cities (among them New York, Boston, San Francisco, and Los Angeles) were meeting regularly to discuss public issues. On the *Dissent* forums, see Lou Anne Bulik, *Mass Culture Criticism and Dissent: An American Socialist Magazine* (New York: Lang, 1993), 74.

24. For the larger context of Howe's stance of liberal anti-communism, see Jennifer Delton, "Rethinking Post–World War II Anticommunism," *Journal of the Historical Society* 10, No. 1 (March 2010): 1–41.

25. John Rodden, *The Politics of Literary Reputation: The Making and Claiming of "St. George" Orwell* (New York: Oxford University Press, 1989), 376.

26. Silone was, for Howe, a literary-political hero much like Orwell, another writer and radical about whom Howe felt no ambivalence—"My favorite living writer," Howe once called Silone, and he perhaps felt a closer fraternal proximity to him than to Orwell, as if Silone were merely a slightly older intellectual big brother (quoted in Gerald Sorin, *Irving Howe: A Life of Passionate Dissent* [New York: New York University Press, 2002], 161). Silone—unlike Trotsky or Orwell, Howe's other literary-political admirations—published in *Dissent*.

In light of the attention throughout this book to "secret intelligence" and the "shadow life" of the profiled subjects, the ironies of Howe's hero worship of Silone warrant mention here. In his essay on Silone, originally published in 1956, Howe acknowledged Silone as an exemplar of the conscientious, responsible, outspoken dissident intellectual who lived on "an intellectual margin." (Perhaps this phrase served as the germ for the title of Howe's autobiography, *A Margin of Hope* [San Diego: Harcourt Brace Jovanovich, 1982].)

I believe Silone represented for Howe a model of how to "dissent" in "this age of conformity." Howe came in fact to see himself as a kind of Jewish American Silone: "The man who will not conform," Howe characterized him, adding explicitly that Silone "is a dissenter." Howe elaborated this idea in terms that further suggest veiled autobiography: "His own attitude toward socialism was to retain the values, even if he could not retain the doctrine. Silone's demand, at once imperious and relaxed, was that others would share with him a belief in the recurrent possibility of goodness." Howe calls Silone "a luminous example" of "a patient writer, one who has the most acute sense of the difference between what he is and what he wishes." Howe proceeds in terms that portray Silone's heroes—and their author—on a level of heroic living that Howe yearns to reach in his moments of utopian reverie:

> The hero of Silone's fiction feels that what is now needed is not programs, even the best Marxist programs, but examples, a pilgrimage of good deeds. Men must be healed. They must be stirred to heroism rather than exhorted and converted. Unwilling to stake anything on the future, he insists that the only way to realize the good life, no matter what the circumstances, is to live it. The duality between the two heroes, between the necessity for action and the necessity for contemplation, between the urge to power and the urge to purity is reflected in Silone's own experience as novelist and political leader. In his own practices as an Italian socialist, he is forced to recognize that the vexatious problem of means and ends involves a constant tension between morality and expediency.

This tension between the attractions of power and purity was one that Howe also carried throughout his life—as a radical who wrote for Henry Luce and *Time*, as a critic of conformist bourgeois life who became a chaired professor of English, as a culture warrior contemptuous of kitsch and lowbrow literature who worked at Paramount Studios in Hollywood, and so on. Howe obviously found inspiration in Silone's public example of how to creatively maintain and balance these oppositions.

What then would Howe have had to say about the shocking revelations about his hero that began to appear after his death in 1993—Silone's preference for means to ends and his choice of expediency over morality as an Italian socialist? Silone's radical credentials and noble image have been soiled by evidence discovered in the 1990s, in the files of the Italian fascist secret police, that he was a fascist informant in the 1930s. Other documents establish that Silone was knowledgeable about CIA funding of the Congress for Cultural Freedom and other anti-Soviet cultural activities of the Western intelligence services in the "cultural Cold War"—activities that Howe castigated in "This Age of Conformity" and in *Dissent*'s pages throughout the 1950s and 1960s. In light of these findings, Howe's praise of Silone sometimes rings most ironically: "The memory of [Silone's] refusal to accommodate himself to the fascist regime stirred feelings of bad conscience among literary men who had managed to become more flexible. Alas, men of exemplary stature are often hard to accept. They must seem a silent rebuke to those who had been less heroic or more cautious."

Quotations from Irving Howe, "Silone: A Luminous Example," in *Decline of the New* (New York: Harcourt, Brace, and World, 1970), 284, 285–87, 288, 290. The essay was first published as "Silone and the Radical Conscience," *Dissent* 3 (Winter 1956): 72–75. It was revised and reprinted in *Politics and the Novel* (New York: Meridian, 1957) as well as in *Decline of the New*.

27. These concerns were surely heightened by the unrest in Eastern Europe after the failed Hungarian Revolution in October 1956.

28. See Bulik, *Mass Culture Criticism*, 74.

29. Agents also monitored Howe's lecture, "A Crisis in the Communist World," delivered on November 16, 1957, at the YWCA in Detroit.

30. The indictments and trials that ended in 1957 came as the result of a series of Supreme Court decisions. In *Yates v. United States* (354 U.S. 298 [1957]), the Court ruled 6–1 that the convictions of numerous party leaders were unconstitutional, distinguishing between advocacy of an idea for incitement and the teaching of an idea as a concept. In *Watkins v. United States* (354 U.S. 178 [1957]), the Court ruled 6–1 that defendants could use the First Amendment as a defense against "abuses of the legislative process."

31. On April 14, 1959, the Detroit office closed Howe's file, and other regional offices did likewise. At this time, Howe was lecturing at Wayne State University. His file was first declassified in August 1985, with additional material declassified in September 1997.

EPILOGUE: THE ORWELLIAN FUTURE?

1. See John Rodden, *Every Intellectual's Big Brother: George Orwell's Literary Siblings* (Austin: University of Texas Press, 2007). At various times Trilling, Macdonald, and Howe have all been nominated as successors to Orwell both as critic-intellectuals and as public voices. All three have been dubbed by their admirers the "American Orwell." On these matters, see John Rodden, *The Unexamined Orwell* (Austin: University of Texas Press, 2011), especially part 1, "If the Mantle Fits . . ."

2. I have discussed the FBI, State Department, and British dossiers on Orwell and his work in John Rodden, *The Politics of Literary Reputation: The Making and Claim-*

ing of "St. George" Orwell (New York: Oxford University Press, 1989); John Rodden, *Scenes from an Afterlife: The Legacy of George Orwell* (Wilmington, Del.: ISI, 2003).

3. Our ersatz "strength" (like the Nazis' *Macht durch Freude* [Strength through Joy]) makes it easy for propagandists to colonize our minds and spirits. "We shall squeeze you empty," O'Brien declares to Winston in Room 101, and "we shall fill you with ourselves."

As we cruise and surf and scan and click, the Telescreen—the "Apple of Our I(phone)s"—"unpersons" us with no need for primitive contraptions like cages of rabid rats in our faces. Our minds go down the memory hole as we text and twitter in the tonal bath of the I-tune Telescreen Lullaby: "We shall drain you of your identity—and we shall fill you with our hype." All this is not MAD but SAD (Self-Assured Destruction).

I do not mean to jest. In light of these realities, a former contractor with the FBI has written to me that he is even more worried by the domestic security alarmists than by the international terrorists. Even more so than the latter, he fears the possibility of federal overreaction "to the threat of violent acts in the USA. I do not think it improbable that citizens would exchange their civil liberties for promises of security and social benefits." He adds, "There is no shortage of real enemies the government must legitimately defend against. . . . Focusing on one threat to the exclusion of others is a real danger. Also not realizing how these threats interact and relate to one another is dangerous as well."

4. On these issues, see the comments of ex-CIA director Michael Hayden in Paul D. Shinkman, "Former CIA Director: Cyber Attacks Game-Changers Comparable to Hiroshima," *U.S. News and World Report*, February 20, 2013.

5. Quoted in ibid.; also cited in John Seabrook, "Network Insecurity," *New Yorker*, May 20, 2013, 70.

6. David Rothkopf in *Foreign Policy*, cited in Seabrook, "Network Insecurity," 70. Given the April 2015 release of the Pentagon's thirty-three-page cybersecurity strategy document, the "cool war" may heat up very quickly in the near future. The document is a response to discoveries that Russian hackers swept up President Barack Obama's email correspondence during 2014. Although the breach was apparently limited to the White House's unclassified computers, Washington is no longer just "playing defense" but also "developing the malware and other technologies that would give the United States offensive weapons should circumstances require disrupting" networks of such adversaries as the foreign governments of Russia, China, Iran, and North Korea. More than one dozen other countries are "making similar investments" ("Preparing for Warfare in Cyberspace," *New York Times*, April 28, 2015).

The FBI will have the role of first response to threats of cyberaggression, with other government agencies (the NSA, the Department of Homeland Security, the CIA, and the Pentagon) following up with various kinds of offensive cyberoperations. So the Orwellian specter that intelligence operations might shift from the international to the extraterrestrial is no longer sci-fi speculation. A militarized cyberspace is now on the verge of representing a new war front among rival powers. *Star Wars*—or a sinister *E.T.*—is upon us.

7. See Lara Jakes and Darlene Superville, "Obama: Spying Legal, Limited," *Austin American-Statesman*, June 8, 2013. The president was backtracking from his much-quoted promise as a candidate in 2007 to reject "the false choice between the liberties we cherish and the security we provide. I will provide our intelligence and law enforcement agencies with the tools they need to track and take out the terrorists without undermining the Constitution and our freedom" (Al Lewis, "Dirty Bomb Blows Liberty," *Wall Street Journal*, June 9, 2013).

8. "W's Apprentice," *The Economist*, May 18, 2013, 29–30.

9. See, for example, Jürgen Liminski, "Big Brother Obama," *Kirchenpost*, June 15, 2013; Stephan Meetschen, "Der Deutsche Traum vom amerikanischen Messias," *Die Tagespost*, June 20, 2013. The German press, which had greeted Obama during his 2008 presidential campaign as a political "Messiah," "a miracle worker, peacemaker, and ray of hope for a better world," has been particularly disillusioned and derisive since the advent of the NSA scandals in 2013 occasioned by Edward Snowden's disclosures. See again Meetschen, "Deutsche Traum," 9. (Since April 2015, when reports surfaced that German intelligence agencies had also snooped on important European allies, especially France—and shared much of the data with the United States—the German media's harsh critiques of such surveillance activities have focused on Berlin.)

10. Of course, such conjectures are speculative, and as I have warned elsewhere, one should constantly be on guard to distinguish between disinterested inquiry and politically motivated grave robbing—a line all too easy to cross. See John Rodden, "On the Ethics of Admiration—and Detraction," *Midwest Quarterly* 46, No. 3 (2005): 284–98; Thomas Cushman and John Rodden, *George Orwell: Into the Twenty-First Century* (Boulder, Colo.: Paradigm, 2004), 86–95; John Rodden, *Every Intellectual's Big Brother: George Orwell's Literary Siblings* (Austin: University of Texas Press, 2006), 181–91.

11. One of the key intellectual works of the "preventive war school" during the early Cold War era was James Burnham's *The Struggle for the World* (London: Cape, 1947), whose arguments he elaborated further in *Containment or Liberation?: An Inquiry into the Aims of United States Foreign Policy* (New York: Day, 1953). In hindsight, however, Burnham erred gravely in his doomsday prophecies, such as his prediction that "if the communists succeed in consolidating what they have already conquered, then their complete world victory is certain. . . . We are lost if our opponent so much as holds his own" (*Containment or Liberation*, 251, 254). Likewise, his "might is right" ideology of beneficent imperialism, whereby he championed what Orwell once deplored as "hundred percent Americanism," verged on the totalitarian. Burnham wrote that in the struggle with communism, "For us, international law can only be what it was at Nuremberg (and what it would have been at Moscow and Washington if the other side had conquered): a cover for the will of the more powerful" (*Struggle for the World*, 148).

Burnham's language resounds in the rhetoric of a leading contemporary neoconservative, Charles Krauthammer, who writes, "America is no mere international citizen. It is the dominant power in the world, more dominant than any since Rome. Accordingly, America is in a position to reshape norms, alter expectations and create new realities. How? By unapologetic and implacable demonstrations of will" (quoted in R. J. Stove, "British Cold Warriors and the War on Terror," *National Observer*, Summer 2009, 61).

12. John Foster Dulles, "A Policy of Boldness," *Life*, May 19, 1952, 146.

13. Kennan (1904–2005) laid out the case for containment in a famous article in *Foreign Policy* in 1947 that he signed "X." His long-range strategy for blocking the worldwide advance of communism and eventually defeating the USSR proved visionary. Kennan argued that firm containment of Stalinism had "nothing to do with outward histrionics: with threats or blustering or superfluous gestures of outward 'toughness'" (X [George Kennan], "The Sources of Soviet Conduct," *Foreign Affairs*, July 1947, 861). Rather, Kennan saw the Cold War campaign as hinging on patience and on the authenticity and credibility of the West's respect for personal freedom. How true would the "Free" World be to its professed values? "It is the Russians, not we, who cannot afford a world half slave and half free. The contrasts implicit in such a world are intolerable to the fictions on which their power rests. . . . If only one ray of light of individual dignity or human inquiry is permitted to exist, the [Soviet] effort must eventually fail" (cited in David Myers, *George Kennan and the Dilemmas of U.S. Foreign Policy* [New York: Oxford University Press, 1990], 117–18).

14. See Stove, "British Cold Warriors," 61.

15. Orwell died a month before Joseph McCarthy's rise to prominence in February 1950. For this reason, Orwell never referred to McCarthy himself in his work, nor did he ever use the phrase *McCarthyism*. He did not live to witness the rise of McCarthy—and his precipitous fall in mid-1954. But anti-Communist hysteria was building and the Red Scare was already in full swing—fueled by such events discussed in this book as the Hiss-Chambers trial and the activities of HUAC. The paranoid climate of what soon became known as McCarthyism permeated American life. It was the emerging, officially sponsored loyalty campaign to root out "activities" that were "un-American" to which Orwell's phrase referred.

16. The rhetoric of the Bush administration's War on Terror campaign relied on a language of demonology. The Bush White House relied heavily on the use of enemy scapegoats to marshal and maintain support for its two military invasions and dramatic escalations of national security measures. By contrast, the Obama administration made concerted efforts to rebrand rival nations so that there were no longer any "enemies" (e.g., Iran, North Korea, and so on). Of course, if foreign nations deem themselves to be at war with the United States, then it is an idealism of the Panglossian kind not to regard them as enemies.

So American foreign policy during much of the last two decades has ricocheted from one extreme to another, between a Democratic administration seeing no enemies (only misunderstandings) and a Republican administration tending to scapegoat rivals and pursue military rather than diplomatic solutions to further its political agenda. The polar swings have become characteristic of Washington "regime change." They send confusing signals to both our allies and our rivals. Yet they also demonstrate the extreme difficulty of articulating and executing a balanced, rational foreign policy in an ever-more-volatile, perilous geopolitical climate.

INDEX

Supreme Court and, 26, 83, 108–9n20, 124n30

Cleveland, FBI regional bureau in, 22

Cold War, 2, 8, 99n8, 108–9n20, 115–16n29, 123n26, 127n13; Communist Party and, 41, 72, 105n1; FBI and, x, 3, 5, 7, 11, 34, 41, 71–72, 94, 103n9, 111n30, 114–15n8; New York Intellectuals and, 7, 34, 52, 72, 100n12, 101n5; vs. "9/11" and later, 94, 100n12; Orwell and, 2–3, 34, 88, 90–92, 94, 100n12; as Red Scare, x, 7, 27, 85, 127n15

Columbia University, 19, 21, 24, 27, 29, 33–34, 67, 107n9, 109–10n22

communism and communists, 20, 41, 55, 101n5, 108–9n20, 112n33, 122n15, 127n13; Chambers and, 26–27, 113–14n40; Cold War and, 41, 127n13; Columbia University and, 19, 21, 24, 33; Communist Party (CP), 19, 23, 31, 38, 46, 105n1, 105n4, 107n14, 109n21; Hoover and, 24, 41, 42, 46; Kazin and, 30–32, 110–11n29; Macdonald and, 38, 41–42, 46, 72, 75, 78, 117n39; L. Trilling and, x, 14–15, 102n7, 106nn6–7, 108nn18–19, 109–10n22, 113n39

Congress for Cultural Freedom (CCF), 6, 34, 47, 97, 101n5, 102n5, 114n42, 123n26

Cook, Richard, 102n7, 120n7

Denver, FBI regional bureau in, 24

Detroit, FBI regional bureau in, 19, 28, 29, 124n29, 124n31; and Howe, 71, 82–83

Dewey, John, 22, 42, 107n10

Dissent (magazine), 13, 16–17, 48, 72, 74–76, 78, 81–83, 104n27, 123n26

Encounter (magazine), 46, 58, 62, 66, 103n11, 110–11n29, 115n24, 115–16n29; Josselson and, 47–49, 101n5; Kristol and, 46–47, 66; Macdonald and, 46–49, 58, 62, 66, 115n24, 115–16n29

Federal Bureau of Investigation (FBI), 7, 10–11, 15–16, 53, 110–11n29, 114n41, 125–26n6; and Cold War, 71–72; vs. "egghead" intellectuals, 5, 17, 111n30; and *Experiment in Terror*, 49, 56; and Howe, 31–32, 38–40, 49, 71–79, 81–83, 120nn3–4, 120n7; as "Keystone Cops," 34; and Macdonald, 37–46, 49–51, 55–60, 64–68, 104n26, 110n28, 116–17n37; and security, 10–11, 14, 16, 26, 32, 40, 43, 71; Security Index of, 40, 46, 65, 72, 75, 80–81; and L. Trilling, 13–15, 21–28, 30–35, 102n7, 105n1, 108n16, 111n30.

See also national security; *entries for specific regional bureaus*

freedom. *See* civil liberties

Freedom of Information Act (FOIA), 6, 10, 97, 103n12

Goldman, Eric, 55, 62, 99n10, 116n36, 117nn42–43; White House Festival of the Arts, 54, 60, 63

Hayden, Michael, 89, 125n4

Hellman, Lillian, 26, 54, 109n21

Hemingway, Ernest, xi, 13, 39, 77, 114n41

Hersey, John, 26, 60

Heston, Charlton, 62, 64, 117–18nn47–48

Hiss, Alger, 23, 100n12, 107nn14–15, 108n19

Hiss-Chambers case, 19, 23, 30, 107n13, 127n15

Hitchens, Christopher, 40, 105n29

Hitler, Adolf, 42, 87, 119n1

Hollywood Ten, 26, 34, 74, 109n21

Hook, Sidney, 6, 22, 42, 47, 49, 66, 106n6, 121n11

Hoover, J. Edgar, 3, 24, 27, 93, 114n1; and Macdonald, x, 37, 41–46, 49–50, 56, 60

Horenstein, Irving (aka Irving Howe), 71, 75–76, 79, 81, 83–84, 120n3, 121n13, 122n19

House on 92nd Street, The (film), 43

House Un-American Activities Committee (HUAC), 23, 72–73, 110–11n29, 120n7

Howe, Irving: at Brandeis University, 75, 77–78, 82, 122n21; and Jewishness, 6, 14–15, 123–24n26; and *Labor Action*, 76, 82, 122n15; *A Margin of Hope*, 17, 77, 105n30, 123–24n26; and *Mass Culture Criticism and Dissent*, 122n23, 124n28; and *New International*, 76, 90; *Politics and the Novel*, 77, 123–24n26; at Princeton University, 77, 80, 104n28; and socialism 77, 80–83, 123–24n26; at Stanford University, 70, 75, 78; *The U.A.W. and Walter Reuther*, 80; at University of Michigan, 77, 82; at Wayne State University, 82, 124n31

Independent Socialist League (ISL), 71–73, 75–76, 80, 82, 119n1, 121–22nn14–15, 122n20

Javits, Jacob K., 55, 60

Johnson, Lyndon, 32, 56, 110nn27–28, 110–11n29; and JFK, 28, 50; and Vietnam War, 50–55, 60–63; White House Festival of the Arts, 21, 28, 102n7

Josselson, Michael, 106nn5–6, 115n23, 115–16nn25–27, 117n29; and CCF, 6, 47, 97, 101n5; and *Encounter*, 47–49, 101n5

Kazin, Alfred, 53–54, 106n8, 112n32, 113n39; FBI dossier, 5–7, 27, 30–32, 73, 102n7, 110–11n29, 120n7
Kennan, George, 60, 127n13
Kennedy, John F., 28, 50, 56, 60, 87, 118n53
Kristol, Irving, 6, 47, 66, 115n26
Krupnick, Mark, 21, 105n2, 106n7

Labor Action (newspaper), 76, 82, 122n15
Leninism and Leninists, 42–43, 61
Liberal Imagination, The (L. Trilling), 28, 30, 108n19, 110n26
Los Angeles, FBI regional bureau in, 24, 122n23
Luce, Henry, 38, 57, 67, 123–24n26

Macdonald, Dwight: "America! America!" 48, 115–16n29; and Communist Party, 38, 41–42, 46, 72, 75, 78, 117n39; as a "Critical American," 16, 67, 74, 104n25, 115n24, 117n41; *Discriminations*, 65, 116n35, 118n52; and *Dissent*, 13, 48, 115n25; drinking problem of, 50, 58; and *Esquire*, 49–50, 56, 64; and *Fortune*, 38, 55, 57, 108n18; *Memoirs of a Revolutionist*, 65, 117n38; *A Moral Temper*, 104n25, 114n2; and socialism, 13, 16, 38, 40, 42, 76; and *Twentieth Century*, 48, 59, 104n25, 115n24; writer's block of, 50
Managerial Revolution, The (Burnham), 90
Marxism and Marxists, 11, 17, 21–22, 78, 98n3, 104–5n29, 106n8, 113–14n40
Masters of Deceit (Hoover), 46
McCarthy, Joseph, 17, 24, 41, 55, 72, 74, 83–84, 127n15
McCarthy, Mary, 6, 22, 54, 59, 100n1
McCarthyism, 3, 7, 16–17, 27, 34, 72, 75, 88, 91
Miami, FBI regional bureau in, 71
Middle of the Journey, The (L. Trilling), 27, 30–32, 106n6, 107n12, 107–8n15, 108n19, 113n37, 114n40; Chambers and, 13, 19, 23–25, 108n16
Miłosz, Czesław, 39–40
Mission to Moscow (film), 42
Moscow, 21–22, 26, 42, 106n7, 107n10

Nation (magazine), 22, 30, 118–19n62
National Committee for the Defense of Political Prisoners (NCDPP), 19, 21, 105n2, 106n7
national security, x, 3–4; and elastic guidelines, 12; and FOIA, 10, 12; and the intellectual Left, 11, 16–17, 26, 32; and "normal Intelligence," 5–6; policies as threat to constitutional rights, 39–40, 84–85, 89, 92, 94, 125n3; and Smith Act, 26
National Security Agency (NSA), 4, 89, 99n11, 103n17, 125–26n6, 126n9
Nazism and Nazis, 34, 43, 45, 91, 100n1, 106n4, 125n3
Newark, FBI regional bureau in, 71, 77, 104n28
New Haven, FBI regional bureau in, 24
New International (magazine), 76, 90
New Left, xi, 39, 74, 101n5, 120–21n8
New Republic (magazine), 22, 30, 118–19n62
New York, FBI regional bureau in, 22–24, 41, 43, 45–46; and Howe, 71, 78; and L. Trilling, 19, 27–28
New Yorker (magazine), 45–46, 55–57, 65, 110n26, 118–19n62, 125n5
New York Intellectuals, 12, 14, 61, 87, 97, 99n7, 100n1, 100n12, 101n3; and Cold War, 5, 7, 34, 52, 72, 100n12, 101n5; as "eggheads," 5, 17, 111n30; FBI surveillance of, 6–7, 13–14, 21, 34, 66, 72; and *Partisan Review*, 14, 52, 99n7, 100n1, 101n3, 101n5
New York Review of Books (magazine), 54, 63, 110n28
New York Times, 27, 46, 54, 60, 100n12, 110–11n29
Nineteen Eighty-Four (Orwell), 2, 4, 87–88, 90–94, 100n12, 105n29
Northbridge, Clifton Bennet, 43–45, 115n18
Novack, George, 22, 107n10

Orwell, George, 15, 66, 87, 88–95, 100n12, 119n63, 123n26, 127n15

Partisan Review (*PR*; magazine), 77, 87, 95, 97, 98n6, 99nn6–7, 101n3, 112n35, 121–22n14. See also New York Intellectuals
Patriot Act, 12, 32
Philadelphia, FBI regional bureau in, 24, 51
Plastrik, Stanley, 71, 74, 78, 122n15
politics (magazine), 38–46, 57, 66, 68, 115n18, 115n21, 115n24, 118–19n62, 122n15; and anarchism and anarchists, 38, 40, 43–44, 56–57, 118–19n62; Hoover and, 41–46, 56, 60; Howe and, 16, 74, 76; Macdonald and, 16, 38, 40–42, 46, 56, 65, 76, 115n24

Popular Front policy, 22, 44, 91
PR. See *Partisan Review* (*PR*; magazine)
Princeton University, 77, 80, 104n28
privacy, x, 5, 6, 40, 72–73, 81, 88–89, 92–93;
  Constitution and, 3–4, 10, 41, 85, 124n30

Rahv, Phillip, 6, 27, 38, 49, 57
Rebel in Defense of Tradition, A (Wreszin),
  60, 104n25, 114n2
Red Scare, x, 7, 27, 85, 127n15
Revolutionary Workers League (RWL),
  21–23, 30, 107n11
Rorty, James, 22
Roth, Phillip, 31, 52, 54, 111n31
Rothko, Mark, 54, 60

San Francisco, FBI regional bureau in, 24,
  49, 122n23
Schapiro, Meyer, 22
Schrecker, Ellen, 102n9, 114–15n8
Schwartz, Delmore, 31, 98n6, 99n6, 112n35
security. *See* national security
Security Index, FBI's, 40, 46, 65, 72, 75,
  80–81
Smith Act (Alien Registration Act), x, 26,
  72, 74–75, 79, 83, 108–9n20
Snowden, Edward, 4, 99n11, 100n12, 126n9
Sobell, Morton, 46
socialism and socialists, 31, 106n8, 123–
  24n26
Socialist Workers Party (SWP), 16, 22, 26,
  38, 42, 46, 80, 107n10, 119n1
Soviet Union (USSR/Russia), 19–20, 40, 57,
  98n3, 105–6n4, 106n5, 110–11n29, 121n10,
  125–26n6; Cold War and, 27, 34, 71, 90,
  123–24n26; Howe and, 17, 71, 76, 80,
  123–24n26
Stalin, Joseph, 17, 31, 57, 74, 87, 90
Stalinism and Stalinists, 6, 30, 40–42, 44,
  71–72, 90–91, 113n37, 127n13
Stanford University, 70, 75, 78
Stevenson, Adlai, 5, 17, 104–5n29
St. Louis, FBI regional bureau in, 71
Struggle for the World, The (Burnham), 90,
  126–27n11

terrorism, 2, 4, 88, 92; and ISIS, 89, 90; and
  "9/11" (September 11, 2001), ii, 89, 100n12
Thomas, Norman, 22, 42
Time (magazine), 26, 63–64, 105–6n4,
  123–24n26

Tragedy of Lyndon Johnson, The (Goldman),
  60, 116n36, 117nn42–43, 118n51
Trilling, Diana, 6, 20, 29, 47, 106nn5–6,
  110n26, 112n36
Trilling, Lionel; and Jewishness, 6, 14–15, 21,
  27–28; *The Liberal Imagination*, 28, 30,
  108n19, 110n26; and National Committee for the Defense of Political Prisoners
  (NCDPP), 19, 21, 105n2, 106n7; "Our
  Country and Our Culture" (*PR* symposium), 31, 112n34. See also *Middle of the
  Journey*
Trotsky, Leon, 16–17, 19, 22, 28, 76, 107n10,
  123n26
Trotskyism and Trotskyists, 14, 19, 21, 33,
  106n7, 107n11, 111n30; Howe and, 16–17,
  31, 71–72, 76–78, 82–83, 120n7; ISL and,
  71–72, 76, 82, 119n1, 122n20; Macdonald
  and, 16, 38–39, 42–46, 52, 55, 58, 71–72;
  Partisan Review and, 77, 121–22n14
Twentieth Century (magazine), 48, 59,
  104n25, 115n24

University of Michigan, 77, 82
U.S. Constitution. *See under* civil liberties;
  national security

Vietnam War, 50–55, 60–63, 107n10

Wallace, Henry, 15, 45, 55, 117n38
Warren, Robert Penn, 27, 54
Washington, D.C., FBI regional bureau in,
  24, 42–44
Watson, Marvin, 55, 120n7
Wayne State University, 82, 124n31
White House Festival of the Arts, 21, 50, 52,
  60–64; Goldman and, 54, 60; Johnson
  and, 28, 50, 60, 102n7, 120n7; Kazin and,
  102n7; Lowell and, 53, 54; Macdonald and,
  x, 13, 28, 32, 50, 52, 61–62, 64, 120n7; L.
  Trilling and, 21, 28
Wilson, Edmund, 14, 22, 42, 106n7
Wilson, Woodrow, 87, 118n53
Winchell, Walter, 44
Workers Party (WP), 75–76
Wreszin, Michael, 60–61, 104n25, 114n2,
  115n24, 115n28, 118n49, 118n56

Yaddo, 106n6, 110–11n29

Zanuck, Darryl, 43

JOHN RODDEN has taught at the University of Texas at Austin and the University of Virginia. He has published four other books on the New York intellectuals.

The University of Illinois Press
is a founding member of the
Association of American University Presses.

University of Illinois Press
1325 South Oak Street
Champaign, IL 61820-6903
www.press.uillinois.edu